BECOMING A MILLIONAIRE IN REAL ESTATE

HOW TO GO FROM BROKE TO MILLIONS IN REAL ESTATE WITH OR WITHOUT MONEY

UEBERT ANGEL

D1070304

Disclaimer

About the Book

"Becoming a millionaire in Real Estate" acts as a guru for you while you set out to make money in the real estate market. You're at the right place if you need to make big bucks without waiting for huge capital investments.

This book not only helps you in navigating the world of real estate, but will shape your entire mindset of financing and earning capitals from scratch. It introduces you to the low-risk, high-yield real estate investment machine that will bring in fast cash and big profits.

By mastering the techniques given in this book, you can multiply your wealth and minimize your risks of failure and loss. Most importantly, this book will be just the source you need in order to build and maintain a strong investment portfolio.

The best part is: This little informational key here, if used correctly, will take you to a door which will make you go from broke to millions! You heard this right; the pages below contain expert analysis and tips of building a mountain of dollars, even when you have no money to start with.

So, are you ready? Turn the pages to start your exciting trip in the profit making world of real estate.

Table of Contents

Chapter 1

Real Estate—the Best Way to Earn Millions

I am a multimillionaire going towards the billionaire status and I must say, that goal alone used to be fulfilling until I matured and realized that nothing is as fulfilling as empowering someone else to become financially secure. You see, learning how to get wealthy through real estate is as much an "art" as it is a "science"- but both easy. I assure you, its not a mystery that only the Frodo's of this world can decode, nope, its not. Not even close!

Why Real Estate?

Let me say, God is no longer creating any more land but only buyers of the land. With babies born at the rate of 130 million per year, meaning to say demand is greater than supply so whoever owns real estate has the upper hand. You may argue with how I did my statistical analysis by saying there are also deaths so the figures cancel themselves out, but you would be dead wrong. You have to understand that the UNICEF figures I gave you above say 130 million are born per year, but according to Quora the number of deaths per year are only half that, meaning you still have a 65 million increase in the number of human beings above the 7 billion that are already on earth at the writing of this book, and that means a 65million increase in land buyers per year. That's huge and scary but appetizing for people like me who supply the land.

As for land, it is actually reducing in size due to rising sea levels, so demand is high and supply is diminishing. When I got those figures I decided to be the one supplying. You got it now. Easy Money!

Now you understand why I am in real estate. In a nutshell it is that high demand for real estate and low supply of it that got me there. I understood the law of supply and demand. You might ask, what is that?

What is the 'Law Of Supply And Demand'
The law of supply and demand is the theory explaining the interaction between the supply of a resource and the demand for that resource. The law of supply and demand defines the effect the availability of a particular product, in this case land, and the desire (or demand) for that product has on price. Generally, a low supply and a high demand increases price, and in contrast, the greater the supply and the lower the demand, the lower the price tends to fall. However as aforementioned, land is now diminishing and numbers of buyers increasing so price is great in real estate!

Why you must be thinking about Real Estate
For starters the road you drive your car on is real estate, the work place you go to daily is real estate, the car park you park your car on is real estate, the restaurant you eat in is real estate, the gym you go to is real estate, the holiday places you visit are real estate, the airport you fly from is real estate, the mall you like to shop in is real estate, the house you sleep in and even the toilet you relieve yourself in is real estate. So everywhere you look you see real estate.

I know the idea of investing in real estate might have popped up in your mind while you were searching for ways to earn quick money, or simply to invest your existing assets for the sake of building on your cash pyramid. In any case, you are now considering investing your precious time in this book because you have a clear idea of the powerful impact real estate has on your financial future.

So, Why Do You Need To Invest in Real Estate?
As I have proven in my introductory paragraphs above, real estate is one of best investment platforms you can get your hands on. I have met and taught many people who come limping injured from the stock market and other failed business ventures, and led them straight into millions through real estate. They feel the need of real estate investments in their portfolio because they have seen a rising number of people profiting from it.

Notice, it offers low-risk opportunities, along with the fact that you don't necessarily have to be a genius to invest in property. You can even start it with the lowest capital possible. You can even use other people's money and use zero of your own.

I don't believe in owning your own house as a great investment and I know a lot of people want to own their own house. That might shock you since I am talking about real estate, but where you would be wrong is thinking I am talking about real estate when I am talking about making money through real estate. Understand that having a house you live in is not an investment in my book. It is a liability. To me anything that doesn't earn you money is a liability and should be gotten rid of.

This book is really here to talk about making millions through real estate and not cage your money in a house you buy and live in. Get this, when you own a house the real person who gets paid is the one who sold you the house you live in and not you. He had a piece of land and sold it to you for a profit at the current value or more so you got fleeced and he or she got paid!

Real estate has nothing to do with showing off with a nice house you live in before you make money. There are times I used to live in a very small house but I had gotten over 100 properties in my name. The focus was on making millions before I got my own mansion so to speak. I was driven and still am but now I can afford to be in a multimillion dollar home because I made the money. I made the millions. I smile all the way to the bank. I am getting paid. Hope you are following what I am saying!

Real estate is the most valuable outlet of earning easy money and is miles better than the fluctuating stock market. With real estate you never stop earning even after retirement.

Here are some of the core benefits:

Cash Flows which are tax free

In the real estate business, the cash flow is tax free. You heard that right. Being an investor, you will never have to pay tax on the appreciation or capital you make, until you decide to sell it. Even if you're exchanging your capital, there is no tax involved. Being an investor, you can also borrow money from a bank and pay zero tax on the loan. The plus point is that you're able to keep the assets and your tax deductions that come with it

Appreciation of Assets

The appreciation you get for your assets might be the top reason why people choose to invest in real estate, but that is not all. You can't claim that you don't have your hopes up high while investing in property but you don't have to keep your fingers crossed because in real estate, you're in 100% control of your assets.

Inflation is another factor which plays a major role in appreciation. It's a primary requirement for appreciation and fortunately for people like us, it's always on the mount. It is always rising.

After more than 75 years John D. Rockefeller is still considered the richest man in history when you adjust for inflation. According to the New York Times as of 2007, his net worth reached $192 Billion. Compare this with Bill Gates whose fortune is only $82 Billion. This shows how enormous the fortune of John D Rockefeller actually was. Only Commodore Vanderbilt and John Astor have even come close with $143 Billion and $116 Billion.

Rockefeller at one time controlled 90% of the nation's oil and his fortune was approximately 1.5% of the nation's economy. That is legacy wealth. Wealth that is hard to lose or destroy. Even though all his wealth was made from oil, he still attributes major fortunes being made in land or real estate. That is a powerful statement. What I am going to discuss here is one of the reasons why building wealth in real estate can create legacy wealth for you and your family. Wealth that can last for many generations if it is managed properly. Interestingly enough this is also one of the least understood benefits of owning real estate.

Buying Low—Selling High
The **"Buy low, sell high"** is another very famous advantage of real estate. It's a basic fundamental economic rule and no economist agrees otherwise. Even though people may say that an investor is asking for a very high profit, it's worth waiting for. There will always be someone who wants your property. You just have to invest in property at the time of depreciation and wait for the right time to gather sales and sell it.

I have some properties in London in the tune of millions so you can imagine that I did my practical and experiential analysis. Although my acquisitions are not in the too distant past I want to show you something starting from way before my birth. For instance as of

1975, London houses have added double the value of the average property in the UK. The London market is distinct because it's basically a separate city-state from the rest of the UK, and because it is surrounded by an unbuildable "green belt," which makes it more like an island than a conurbation and that in another way makes the properties there valuable and so gave me the reason to choose that city for investment. However the main point here is after I chose the city I waited for the prices to go very low and I jumped in because I knew with all these other factors, London was to rise and I have since seen my real estate investment there double in no time.

The benefit of Leverages

Leverage is an investment strategy of using borrowed money to generate outsized investment returns. For example most people will go to an automobile dealership and admire the new vehicles available to purchase. And after being sweet-talked by an enthusiastic sales man you leave the forecourt with a brand new car, even though they can't even afford to pay for that car in cash. What just happened? If the cost of the vehicle is $30,000 and you only have $3,000 in cash and $27,000 in borrowed money in exchange for the vehicle, the buyer's cash outlay was only 10% of the vehicle's purchase price. Using borrowed money to pay 90% of the cost enabled the buyer to obtain a significantly more expensive vehicle than what could have been purchased using only available personal cash. Instead of driving around in a battered $2,000 banger, the buyer is cruising around town in a shiny new car, having used leverage to acquire a better vehicle than he or she could have purchased using only available cash on hand.

Using leverages to invest is one of the greatest benefits of real estate. Getting money couldn't be more fun than it becomes in the real estate bandwagon. A real estate investor who has $50,000 in cash could use that money to buy one home valued at $50,000. If that home could be quickly sold for $55,000, the investor would have gained $5,000. If that same investor used the original $50,000 in cash to put a $5,000 down payment on 10 different homes valued at $50,000 each, financed the rest of the money, and then sold all 10 homes for $55,000 each, the investor's profit would have been $50,000 - an astounding 100% return on investment. Even if all you have is $5000 there is nothing that stops you from making a down payment on a property for $50,000 resell for $55,000 you still make your 100% return on investment. I have done it and made a few millions on it and I did this in South Africa not even in these first world countries so I know its possible in any economy so to speak.

Generally, a down payment of up to 20% of the purchase price can be made, and the rest can be financed. This gives you leverage, meaning that you can invest in different types of properties with less money down, helping to build your net worth or income that you could make off the properties.

Depreciation
This is another benefit which is often underestimated because people focus more on regular cash flows and appreciations. When you have owned some property for a longer period of time, it's called depreciation. It helps you to gain an income tax deductions which allows you to recover the cost of a certain property.

This is done by many property investors in America. This is what I call sleeping value!

It's easier than stocks
There is just something about Real estate. It is something that you can physically touch and feel. It's a tangible good and that what makes it feel more real. To set your feet in the stock market, you've got your work cut out for you, you need to hire someone who knows about it inside out, someone who understands the trading system.

Half the time you wont even know what they are talking about because of all the financial jargon, and by the time you get to grips with it all, you have lost a fortune. The fund managers and stock brokers have to assist you with the various financial instruments. Before you make any money at all you have people on your payroll demanding even more from the little you have.

On the other hand, the real estate business is basic. People just need to carry out a good research on the locations and properties involved. If you do your homework you always get paid because what you see is what you get, whereas in stock markets its like guess work and sheer gambling. Its like playing Russian Roulette!

People have to live somewhere. It doesn't matter what the economy is doing or how high the unemployment rate climbs, people have to live somewhere. Think about it, if all your money is tied up in stocks and bonds and the market crashes, you don't have a whole lot of options. But if the market crashes and you have a few rental properties, even if you can no longer charge the same amount in rent, people have to live somewhere, making your investment a consistent option. You won't make the same amount of profit as you did in a normal market, but you will be much better suited to weather a financial storm until the market recovers.

A Great Retirement Plan
Once you near retirement, you will realize that you're grateful you invested in real estate. Buying any property and investing in it can help you in the long run. It builds up a healthy cash flow with sales or rent which makes a comfortable retirement plan for you. Your property portfolio can still bring home the butter long after you hang the boots. An exclusive poll of 1,500 people by market research company Consumer Intelligence for *The Observer* found that one in three is relying on property to help provide an income in retirement. A third said they plan to receive retirement income from one or more buy-to-let properties, while more than half, 55%, said they would sell their own home and use the money to pay for retirement.

It is hardly surprising that growing numbers of people are shunning pensions in favour of property. Returns from company and private pension schemes are uncertain as they depend on how investments perform, and your money is locked away until you reach age 55 at the earliest. On retirement, most people then have to use their pension savings to buy an annuity to provide an income for life but, because of increasing longevity and low yields on gilts, these are often poor value so its better to use properties!

Your Companion during Inflations

You can't possibly imagine a time when you will have to pay $5 for a single bar of Kit Kat. This might seem absurd to you at this point in time but this is where we are heading because of the growing inflation. You can't use your stock certificates or your bars of gold during inflation crisis. But as a real estate investor, you can always move into your own property when you need to, sell it, or leave it intact as you please. Moreover, you can only imagine the high rents people will be willing to pay you in such desperate times.

It's always time to smile when you see inflation. Why would I dare say such a thing? While most people fear inflation, as a rental property owner, I look forward to it! When the price of a bar of chocolate or bottle of milk rises, guess what else is going to shoot through the roof? Everything, including rents and my property values! The one thing that won't increase, however, is my fixed-rate mortgage payment. As inflation pushes the cost of living higher and higher, my cash flow will only increase. This is why real estate is often called "a hedge against inflation." When inflation hits. I'm ready and I am happy as I will be smiling straight to the bank!

Chapter 2

Real Estate Categories

While many of you already know that real estate is one of the oldest and most popular asset classes, what some don't realize is just how many different types of real estate investments you can make. To go from handyman to a real estate tycoon, you must understand the market and categories to make strong real estate gains in.

Each type of real estate investment has its own potential benefits and pitfalls, including unique quirks in the cash flow cycle, lending traditions, and standards of what is considered appropriate or normal so it isn't unusual to see someone build a fortune by learning to specialize in a particular niche.

There are three categories of real estate

1. Residential

Residential real estate consists of houses and town-homes which are both developed and undeveloped. This is the most common type of investment and most of you will be familiar with this one.

2. Commercial

Commercial real estate includes large apartment units, office and warehouse spaces. It also consists of large retail shopping centers.

Their down payments are usually larger and they are also more profitable in terms of cash flow.

3. Industrial
This type of real estate includes big manufacturing industries, mines, farms, car washes and other special purpose real estate that generates sales from customers who temporarily use the facility. Industrial real estate investments often have significant fee and service revenue streams.

Tips for Investing in Real Estate
Once you have decided you want to start real estate investing, getting your toes wet might be a challenging situation. To make you familiar with the real estate world, here are some major guidelines for making investments in real estate.

Use some of these expert tips to embark on an exciting real estate journey which will guide you towards your financial freedom and your multi millionaire status.

Knowing Your Real Estate Calculations

In real estate, everything can turn into a profit for you. Unfortunately, if you aren't careful, the same statement can be true for the losses as well. You have to know your real estate math in order to keep generating a healthy and regular cash flow.

Understanding Real Estate Mathematics

You don't have to be a university student who has a calculus major to grasp real estate math. In real estate, calculating your cash flow is pretty easy.

Income: The amount of money you earn from your property.
Expenses: The money that you spend on investment. For instance, the loan payments and maintenance or garbage bills of your property.
Cash Flow: Cash flow is simply put, the money that is left over with you after you have paid all the expenses from your total income.
(Cash Flow= Income - Expenses)
Simpler than grade 5 mathematics, isn't it?

Treading with Caution

In the world of real estate, you will need to make deliberate, calculating moves to earn big money. Your goal must be to maximize the returns while minimizing the risks involved.

Be Careful

➣ Consider real estate investment as a business and treat it as one.
➣ Know the right time to make a deal.

- Know when to refuse a lousy offer and be bold to reject offers when you don't feel good about signing them.
- Don't walk into the short term loan traps. Be aware of the scammer/lenders that turn out to be sharks in the ocean of real estate.
- Make sure you have a consistent cash flow.
- Wait for your investment to turn fruitful. Don't make haste for the "Quick Money" thing.
- Be very shrewd while selecting your locations.
- If the values drop, choose to wait until it rises up again, rather than selling your property on high tax.
- Talk with other investors and real estate experts.
- Find a good bank or mortgage broker to finance your real estate investing.

Good versus Bad Houses

The real estate world of property owning is divided into good houses and bad houses.

There are some properties which come to you on lease; the lease assets are usually pretty, needing no repair work. The bright side of these is that you have to place them for rent without any investment from your pocket.

On the other hand, the ugly houses come with the headache of additional repairs. They need to be rehabbed before you can earn money from them. But the plus point of getting your hands on such deals is that they come to you very easily at discounted prices.

In my formative years as a budding real estate investor I bought many of these but before that I had befriended a lot of tradesmen, people who had skills in decoration, plumbing and even plastering so it was easy for me because after every purchase I would call these guys to work with me for less during weekends, and since we were close they didn't charge a lot to fix my houses. I have since helped some of these guys to become millionaires too in properties and since I never told them I 'used' them I guess now they will have to know it now that this book is out. So you have my secret, if you meet them don't tell them!

As you can clearly observe, both of these categories have their respective advantages and disadvantages. You should debate which kind will work the best for you and provide more cash flow to make the choice.

Produce a Win-Win Situation
With real estate, you get to create a win-win situation between you and the person you are negotiating with.

Some sellers, even when they are desperate to sell, aren't willing to budge on their rates. You can always explain the worth of their property to them and settle on a number which is satisfactory for both of you. If not, you can always find someone who is willing to make a deal with you.

Remember in negotiations any person who says the figure first is the one who loses. It is what I know and that's my rule of thumb. I never give you my figure because it might be bigger than what you were intending to sell your property for and if it is higher I can still lower the price below the one I want and will always meet in between, and that in-between is usually the real price I wanted it for.

Also remember that in real estate there are always places which you might want to look for in order to locate motivated sellers rather than jump into negotiation with anyone who comes up. Sales agent at the time of selling a property are not even 'human' they are money and commission driven.

For those less religious here is a joke told about a real estate agent.

What is the difference between a sperm and a real estate agent? The answer is simple. A sperm has 1 in 250000 chances of becoming a human than a real estate agent trying to get his commission.

So understand that you do the hunt for bargains before you start hearing all kinds of agents because all they want is a commission and you have to get it. They are at work and they have to get paid and you are their commission ticket so they develop pit bull tenacity and never will they let go until the fleece you!

Arrange Your Finances

Although pretty obvious, this step can be more complex than you think. Investing in real estate is not as simple as purchasing a house or giving it away. In the case of buying an income generating property, you're never really sure how your tenant will be treating your assets. So, it's really important to have financial stability or be able to get a low interest loan if needed.

For starters, make sure you have enough money to keep paying for any repairs. You will also need a bulk sum set aside for emergency purposes. A water pipe burst or maintenance won't be covered by your insurance provider.

Also, since you may or may not be able to rent out your property, are you sure that you will be able to afford the down payments on the property you have selected, without the rental money?

Remember to begin at the right place

To earn quick money through real estate, you need to understand that entering it with the correct mindset holds importance in every prospect. While entering any industry, you can't expect to wake up transformed into a millionaire overnight. Each sector will require you to start low and then build upon your cash flows. Real estate is no different and you need to begin investing on solid grounds.

For instance, you can easily enter the real estate market by doing the following:

Steps to take while investing in a new property:
- Think about a good money making location.
- Buy a property there that you love.
- Change it to a rental property.
- Remember to invest in something that is worth it, because if you don't, you will have difficulties in maintaining it and attracting tenants for it.
- Buy an old property that you can turn into something profitable, only if you're sure you can bear the expenses of flipping it.
- Even if an asset comes to you cheap, don't ever forget to question yourself as to why you need to invest in it and what good it will bring to you when you own it.
- Buying something cheap and spending double the amount of its purchase on rehabbing it, is a step you should avoid, especially when you're entering the real estate world for the first time.

Chapter 3

Finding Your Real Estate Niche

In real estate, you can start investing, simply with your existing assets if you have them. Even renting out a single room in your house can be a small beginning. The advice for people who want to make money is simple: **"If you want to do it, go ahead and do it!"** You don't have to just have a talk about it, or wonder about the techniques too much. Like I said this is not complicated!

Following this advice can be pretty tough for a vast majority of people though, because taking the final steps towards a real estate venture can be scary and people are often afraid of leaving their comfort zone.

To get out of this phase, you will need to back up and have a look at real estate through a simple magnifying glass, not a telescope. Most importantly, you have to be out looking for your real estate niche.

You can't possibly be all things for all people. While moving forward, you will have to find out what particular segment of the market you can specialize in. Find out the thing that will work best for you, depending on your location and financial regulations.

There are countless opportunities in the property market. You can consider some, from the following real estate niches.

A particular kind of property or housing niche
- Bungalows
- Lofts
- Condos
- Farm houses
- Inns or guest houses
- Luxury homes
- Colonials
- Victorians
- Any other new construction

Niche based on various locations
- Counties
- Suburbs
- Cities
- Neighborhoods
- Subdivisions
- Any particular district or community

Niches that are based on particular buyers and sellers

These include the numerous customers who look for services online. You can look into the following buyers or sellers which include:

- Up-scale buyers
- Fixers
- Seconds home buyers
- First time buyers
- Young couples
- Single men or women
- Retirees
- Adult children who want to move out
- Empty nesters
- Downsizers
- International students
- Overseas buyers
- Foreign investors on U.S. property

Niches depending on your skills and knowledge

If you take out time to focus on your real estate expertise, you can also cultivate some of the following niches.

- Buyers representation
- Eco friendly housing
- Expert in negotiations
- Distressed properties
- Senior's home buying
- Relocation
- Baby boomer programs

Other Real Estate Niches

Some other real estate niches can include farms, ranches and even office buildings. Rentals and moving services also make a nice pair with real estate.

A lot more can be added to this list. What's even better is that several of the above can be combined together to give birth to other exciting real estate niches. In the United Kingdom which I call home I have done several constructions of eco friendly houses due to the financial discounts offered by the government and also how easy it is to get planning permission for such. I have made a killing in that niche!

Developing Your Investment Strategies

You have to figure out what according to you is the best strategy that you can go ahead with? Because for each investor; the "best" might vary. For instance, the best strategy for making money for some people might not even be tolerable for others.

It all comes down to how much capital you have and how much time you can give to this moneymaking venture, and obviously, your location is also playing a major factor in shaping your strategy.

Once you have worked out your comfort zone, go ahead and take whatever niche you choose towards the strategy building phase.

Here are some of the development strategies that are commonly used while investing in real estate.

Working for a certain kind of property

As discussed above, you can't be the jack of all trades otherwise you would be a master of none, so select your type before you invest your money. You will absolutely love working on some strategies and at the same time, others might make you bite your tongue. Luckily, in real estate, unlike stocks, you are given the choice to select your own niche and become a master at it. Moreover, you can even combine a range of choices if you don't want to settle on just a single one.

Focus on your skills and passion

It will be best for you if you turn your passion into your real estate plan. Think about it. Do you have a thing for historic structures? Or do you like modern constructions? Do you enjoy the negotiating phase or would you prefer being a property advisor in your locality?

To put it into a broad spectrum, your strategy must depend on your choice of goals. Find your set of assets, narrow down your selections, and finance your investments like an expert.

Specializing In One Specific Area

If the place you're living in has many large subdivisions, it is important to specialize in one particular subdivision. This strategy has turned out to be very creative and productive for some real estate investors. This is commonly known as "Framing" your area and marketing inside your divisions. This strategy works wonders especially when you're living in a rural area with other small towns around you. You can start specializing from one town and then keep adding more to your plate.

Determining Your ROI (Return of Investment)

Many entrepreneurs estimate their ROI when they are entering real estate. ROI is an accounting term which stands for **"Return on Investment."** In the real estate context, this ROI can be calculated in a variety of ways.

$$ROI = (Gains\ from\ investment\ -$$
$$Cost\ of\ Investment)\ /\ Cost\ of\ Investment$$

This particular method is not fully applicable when there are cost changes in equity. The alternate method would be

$$Cost\ Method\ ROI = Equity\ /$$
$$(Improvements\ and\ purchase\ costs)$$

There is another method named **"Out Of Pocket Way"** to calculate ROI which divides equity by costs of purchases and the loan costs combined.

$$Out\ of\ Pocket\ Way = Equity\ /\ (Costs\ of\ purchase$$
$$and\ improvements\ +\ Loan\ Related\ Costs)$$

There might be some further complications in the determination of ROI when your property is refinanced or a mortgage is taken out. Interests on the loan may increase and the ROI may fall down.

On the other hand, there can also be an increase in it when there is additional property maintenance or tax included.

What Are The Monetary Investment Opportunities In Real Estate?

Previously we focused on the various real estate investment strategies and showed you some niches which should come under your consideration. Once you start focusing on your strategies, you will have to select exactly what investment opportunity you want to go with.

Real estate is a huge industry. There are hundreds of investment opportunities to select from. But, you don't need a hundred to start with, you will just want to focus on one, and then move to the others if you're able to generate a positive cash flow.

The section below shares some real estate investment strategies that are both long term and short term. Have a look at them to see if you can use any of them to produce wealth in the real estate market. I have employed all of them in one way or the other!

Long Term Investments

The long term investment techniques are one of the oldest kinds of investments in real estate. They might be the simplest form of investments that exist. If you have a long profit-making goal, pick this to gain an active long term investment.

Buy and Hold

The "buy and hold" investment is recognized in the real estate world as an effective opportunity to get higher appreciation in the longer run.

Typically, a buy and hold investor is looking for ways to generate wealth by renting out their property and collecting the monthly cash from the tenants. They also do it by simply buying a property and holding on to it until it's sold for fat gains after an extended period of time.

Advantage of buy and holds

- ➤ Buy and hold is the core of real estate investment, which offers multiple significant advantages for the investor.
- ➤ The most obvious advantage of buy and hold is that while you're holding on to your assets or renting your property, your mortgage is being cut down with each passing month, eventually decreasing your principal balance with an increasing amount of equity in the capital.

- By this method, you end up owning the property after some years without paying the mortgage yourself. This works because your rentals can be the source of making the monthly loan payments. And because you owned it from the start, you can calculate the profit for which you can sell it in the market.
- With buying and holding, you have the choice to become an active investor by managing your property yourself or you can hire property management services who handle all your tenants for you. The only thing to ensure would be if your property is being cared for properly or not. If you think you can prove to be a dynamic landlord, buy and hold is the way to go!

Things to remember when investing in buy-and-hold properties

- Always make a healthy deal
  While investing in this long-term strategy, you have to make sure that you're making a healthy deal and not getting yourself into trouble instead.

- Remember the two words "Cash Flow"
  Cash flow is the lifeline of buy and hold, especially if you have bought the property using a mortgage. You simply cannot afford to have the property vacated because you will be the one paying the expenses for it, including the rent. A positive cash flow is extremely important in this method because otherwise, you end up losing money every month.

- Evaluate your risks smartly
  You have to be positive that you are going to regulate all the payments including bills and maintenance costs of the property you have chosen. Being an investor, you must understand each and every deal before finalizing it and making a mistake you will later regret. Many investors don't evaluate the property and underestimate their expenses. This, along with the selection of bad tenants, adds up towards building a failed investment.

- Be confident regarding your research on the investment
  This strategy also requires loads of previous research before you get the deal settled because you don't want yourself caught in the middle of a bad deal with a negative cash flow. Learn all the pros and cons of the real estate market that your property is located in.

- What does a smart investor do in a time of slow gains?
  During a slow gain period, when the real estate market flares up, a smart investor usually stops buying until they are sure about their standing again. They can simply hold on to their assets or sell them. Some investors simply keep living on the cash flow until they are sure about selling it and moving on to their next strategy.

Top Five Cities for Buy and Hold Investing

Investing in buy and holds in some cities of the U.S. where I have made money in may prove to be quite easier as compared to others. This is because some expensive cities offer heavy cash returns that keep the investors happy. However whilst the US is what I am focusing on here Angola, South Africa, Nigeria, Ghana, Kenya and Mozambique are also contenders among other African countries I have not mentioned here. In Europe Britain, Germany, Spain, Italy, Poland etc.

Here are some of the cities that can be ranked as the top five based on their high real estate returns, benefits, and other statistics in the US.

- Atlanta
- Saint Louis
- Las Vegas
- Charlotte
- Washington, D.C.

Now back to buy and hold properties. Not all your buy and hold properties will be similar. There are some single family homes which can be good enough. Multi-family homes will also be a good idea if the investor is living in the same location as their tenants, as they allow you to gain more money and require fewer fixes.

All you do is occupy one part of the house and rent the other part at the value of your mortgage per month meaning you are living in your section for free whilst your good tenant is paying your mortgage or house

loan. Its that simple and you don't need to occupy the best part because all you want is to have financial freedom and financial freedom takes sacrifices.

Short Term Investments

Short term investors are usually those who don't like the idea of holding on to a property. Having no patience to wait for the profits over a longer period of time, they master the art of selling and buying or passively investing in real estate to get their hands busy with the regular cash gains. Here are some short-term investment opportunities in the real estate industry that I am currently making cash from.

Fix and Flips

A popular technique for making money in real estate, flipping is largely promoted through television shows. Fixing and flipping are the art of buying a property at a discount and adding some investments in it to improve its state, and then selling it for a certain amount of profit.

You might have seen those reality TV shows which involve countless "real estate gurus" who teach you how to make millions just by flipping property. Many people might have heard about this strategy of acquiring wealth countless times. Although some TV ads and shows repeatedly claim to help you in gaining quick wealth without any work or money required, this is not as simple as it seems.

Fixing and flipping—buying a property to renovate it and then selling it, is not a get rich quick scheme. This takes loads of hard work, understanding, and experience.

Flipping is similar to the simple model which every other business gains from; "buying low, for selling high." But, in order to sell for a higher amount, you will have to offer something to your customer. The most popular property that you can flip is a single family home.

Here are some tips which will be helping you in successfully flipping houses.

Things to remember when flipping a house
   ➢ **Time—Key aspect in flipping**
      A major aspect in flipping a property is the speed with which you carry out the whole process. A good investor will go out to buy, fix and sell the property in the least time possible. This is done to avoid any additional cost of keeping the property on hold. The expenses of a property include the property taxes, maintenance and utility bills etc. Managing to pull off a whole buy and sell cycle quickly is

the reason why this real estate strategy is called "flipping."

> **The 70% Flipping Rule**
Make sure you're following the 70% rule. This states that an experienced flipper buys a home for 70% of its existing value minus the fixing costs. To understand this rule, take a look at this example:
A property buyer knows that home X, if it was in an excellent condition, must be worth around $100,000. But since it requires $20,000 worth of repairs, a house flipper will buy the property for $50,000 ($100,000 x 70% - $20,000) and go out to sell it for the actual $100,000 once it's fully rehabilitated.

> **Always keep an eye on the ARV**
Once your property is ripe to provide you with the fruits of your hard work, don't forget to re-

evaluate the ARV which is the *"after repair value,"* i.e the price for which you sell the property after repairs. If the market has gone through changes, you might need to adjust your ARV accordingly.

Remember, you should never make the mistake of getting your hands dirty in a fix and flip deal which is costing you more than 70% of your ARV. Always live by this rule. I do.

> **Research**

Doing prior research is critical for your success in flipping. This involves conducting long researches on the location that you have made your target. For starters, you don't want to buy or invest in any area which has little price appreciation, as then, your potential buyer will offer low prices.

> **Evaluating the deal**

Visit your real estate agent and ask them to educate you about the process. It is important to have a fixing plan in your hand which includes all the expenses and profits neatly calculated before you get your hands dirty. Analyze the value of the property and compare it with other properties in the neighborhood.

> **Grow your network**

The most foolproof way to enter flipping is by getting to know other people who are investing in the real estate market of your area. It's enormously important for you to grow your network because, by this, you will be able to get hold of buyers.

> **Build a Fixing Team**
If you're still not sure that you will manage to fix the property in time, always keep a fix and flip team ready by your side. Depending on the amount of rehab required, you have to have extra hands in helping you with the task. However this is expensive to do because you will need salaries for your team. I will tell you what I did to curb those costs. I developed contacts with companies and created a rapport so every time I have a project I call them and we split the profits as opposed to me paying that huge team monthly salaries which is really not a wise business idea!

> **Fixing and Rehabilitation Management**
When it comes to fixing and rehabilitation - Your remodeling is equally essential as your deal making. Never be unrealistic in gauging the rehab costs of a particular property. You will be shocked to see how quickly costs can multiply. Don't forget to include holding costs— taxes, insurance, utilities, mortgage and tithing if you are like me etc.
Another essential move while you are rehabbing, would be keeping the potential buyers in your mind in advance. You don't have to always go overboard with your renovations, but if the buyers are deeming something necessary for your location or your neighborhood, don't forget to include that.

➤ **Don't go for buying extra cheap**
When you see someone offering you a house whose price is too good to be true—it probably is. Do your homework, be diligent Real Estate investment is not for the lazy. Always be careful about keeping just the cheap buying factor in your mind when making a deal. What if it needs more repairs than you can put in? What if the buyers do not see it worthwhile even after the rehab process?

➤ **Do not act as a greedy fellow**
Yes you might have had all the glass doors and windows replaced, and you should be showing them off to customers, but do not start overpricing your property. Being greedy will cost you more in the future as you will end up holding on to your property longer than you can afford to, remember this is simply a business transaction. In cases like this I have always told myself if my margins are right I will shake hands with my buyers and walk away. This is the principle that got me here!
This however, doesn't mean that you have to go under price—simply go along with the existing rates of the locality as a general rule. Remember overpriced real estate will simply stay on the market and unfortunately an extended time in the market raises questions in the buyers. They will start thinking there might be a real problem with your property and that drives the demand down causing you to sell even lower.

You see? Use my principle – if margins are right take the deal and walk away!

> ### How long should it take to Fix and Flip a property?
> Depending on your management and cost financing abilities, the time period required to fix and flip a property might vary. For some people, even with experience, it may take up to six months to flip a property. The ideal time under which you should fix and flip for the top dollar is four months.
>
> Start planning ahead to avoid any hazard and always assume that you will end up owning a property and paying for its expenses longer than you originally thought you will.

The flipping process, also commonly known as rehabbing and retailing, is very exciting and can be used as a tool to generate a cash flow which helps you in paying for your bills or other expenses. If used smartly, with a bit of diligence and common sense, this technique can be a source to providing you with an awesome lifestyle. However, be aware in advance that this is not a "passive" activity. Being an investor, if you choose to stop flipping at a certain point, you might be left empty handed.

AirBnb Investments or Vacation Rentals
"Airbnb" is also a type of buy and hold strategy but it also comes under the short-term rental categories of real estate. **Airbnb** is an online marketplace that enables people to list their homes, find, then rent

vacation homes for a processing fee. It has over 2,000,000 listings in 34,000 cities and 191 countries. Founded in August 2008 and headquartered in San Francisco, California, the company is privately owned and operated.

There has been a rise in the number of Airbnb investors recently, as properties have moved towards being more lucrative, hence providing more income than investments.

Again, while investing in this sector of real estate, you have to be sure about some factors, the most important of them being the location, which will directly play an important role in generating your cash flow.

Things to remember when making an Airbnb investment

Vacation or Airbnb short-term rentals are very hands on. Have a look at some important things you will need to keep in mind when buying or considering an Airbnb investment.

> **What is the location of your property?**
  The first and most important questions to ask yourself are regarding the location of your investment. If your property is located miles away from the hustle bustle of the city, important tourist locations and other landmarks, chances are that you will have difficulties in bookings. Location is everything the value of your property is determined by the location chose and again, do your homework! On the other hand, if your lodging is offering various attractive features to the tourists, you will have a large pool of bookings and customers to select from. For instance, you have to look for investment opportunities near the sea or in the middle of the city where everything from parks to theaters and shopping malls is closer by.
  You should also pay attention to some seasons when you are investing, as there are some particular seasons in a year that offer you more cash flows as compared to others.

> **Getting the license and making tax payments**
  Before putting your property on Airbnb, you will need to acquire permission. Check to see if your property is allowed for hosting or not. In addition to that, your investment property might also require a business license. You may also have to pay the occupancy taxes,

the same that are applied to hotels. It's up to you if you want to pass on this tax to the rental prices or not. Some federal taxes might also be applied to your income, which can be reduced if you deduct your business expenses. Other countries also differ in their regulations so make sure you do your research on how you country treats taxes from airbnb.

> **Will you be able to manage the property?**
Once you have your hands on the property, your next step would be to find your first potential customers, i.e. your tenants. The issue here that can arise is—would you be able to handle the turnover between tenants? If your answer is that you will rent them out for longer terms then it's wise to remind you that your tenants might still come up with numerous requests and issues regarding housing that you would be obliged to answer. If you are on the look out to shuffle between tenants, will you have the time set aside to manage the reservations? Can you ensure that all your clients are satisfied with your respective services from their arrival to their departures?
Being a part of an active Airbnb investment is about being available on a full-time basis; with the various tasks that may need assistance. For instance, you will also be required to hire someone to welcome the guests and take care of the utensils and laundry, if you are unavailable to do it yourself.

- **Are you considering this as a part time investment?**

Airbnb should never be considered as a part-time venture that can be considered as a "passive" investment. If you have problems while managing all of the above things, or you live in a place that is away from your property you must consider hiring someone to keep a regular check on your premises. Just like any other business, real estate requires your full attention if you are focusing on making millions from it.

If you are unable to respond to a guest, within 24 hours of check-in, Airbnb could require you to refund their payments. Forgotten arrivals and canceled reservations might do the same.

I personally have used some online services like Pillow, which helped me in my formative years in the management of some of my Airbnb properties.

Using some latest electronic gadgets like Lockitron can also be effective. These locking apps help you in an opening and closing of the doors of your property with the help of your smartphone or tablet.

- **Can you be active for such an investment? Is the extra income beneficial?**

You will have to make sure you have nice neighbors who are aware that you are juggling rentals. Some people are not very pleased about the fact that there is regular activity near their residence. It's a good idea to be friends with the people near your property to make sure you are kept informed in case an unusual incidence occurs. You have to be positive about carrying on with such kind of an investment considering the amount of profit you are generating.

> ## Deciding between long term or short term lease
Even if you are renting your house for a short term lease, there will be expenses which will eat a significant amount of your profits away. You have to be smart while making the selection of either lease category. An amount of 20 to 30 USD for each hour can be charged for cleaning, let alone the damage costs depending on the location of your rental property.

> ## Balancing the expenses
If your property is in a high profile area, which includes major attractions for tourists, then signing up for this strategy in real estate might be an advantage. Moreover, you can individually approve your potential guests and set your rent prices according to your payable taxes and interest. By the end of the day, if you are successfully making more money than you are spending on the rentals, your investment might have a chance to thrive after all.

Best cities in U.S. for AirBnb Investment
According to Forbes, the most lucrative states which come under the top five places for investing in vacation rentals in the U.S. for the year 2015 are;

The best and worst cities for Airbnb

A ranking of cities by regulation around short-term rentals

● Best ● Worst

Source: R Street

> New York City
> San Francisco
> San Diego
> Miami
> Austin

Top cities in the world in terms of Airbnb investments

According to the Guardian, the capital of France, Paris, has become the number one city in the world in terms of Airbnb investments.

Paris has now more than 40,000 listing which are active on Airbnb. So, yes, if you're thinking of investing in the real estate market of a foreign country, Paris is your way to go.

The next under this most popular list comes New York, with around 34,000 listings. The third city in this category would be London, with an estimate of about 23,000 listings. Almost 80,000 British home owners are earning income by renting part or all of their homes through Airbnb – and the number is doubling by the year.

The popularity of the short-term rentals website was boosted further when the Chancellor gave a £1,000 tax break for people who make money out of property or trading. It meant many Airbnb landlords will escape tax altogether.

Commercial Investments

Who hasn't heard of Donald Trump the famous commercial real estate tycoon, who is now also in the presidential race for the White House at the time of writing of this book? So what do commercial investors exactly do? How are people like Trump so successful at generating so much wealth that today they have goals as big as their skyscrapers?

Commercial real estate investing varies in both style and size, but is ultimately serving one purpose, they all consist of properties which are leased to a variety of businesses.

Generally, when people think about "commercial" investments, they are typically thinking about huge shopping centers, warehouses, big hotels and office spaces. But to explain this term from the highest to the lowest level of opportunities available, let's have a look at the different type of commercial real estate investment ventures. Just a few months ago I managed to increase my commercial property portfolio by $5million within 8 weeks just by applying the principles I have shared in this book.

Industrial

This category is divided into 3 sub industries in which people like to invest.

> **Heavy Manufacturing:** Many large industries and manufacturers fall under this category of commercial real estate. These industries are those which produce heavy customized machinery for the target users. These properties at times also require major renovations in order to fit different tenants. A significant thing to consider might be that industrial properties tend to be occupied by one tenant at a time, which adds a certain level of risk to the property.

> **Bulk and Flex Warehouses:** Bulk warehousing is normally very large and consists of a space of about 50,000-1,000,000 square feet. These properties are often used for product distribution and are accessible for large vehicles and trucks who want to use the highways for transportation. On the other hand, Flex space is any property that can be easily converted to meet the needs of both industrial and office spaces.

> **Light assembly:** The simple structures as compared to industrial manufacturing fall under this. The properties in the light assembly are easily reconfigured for typical usage. They may include storage, office spaces, and product assembly.

➤ Office

Office properties are usually classified into three categories. Class A, B or C. These classifications are largely relative in terms of their context. The A class include properties which are in the best location with the best construction. Class B might not have the desired property, but still have high-class construction and of course, the rest of them fall under Class C.

There are some office spaces which are located in CBC (Central Business District). These districts are in the heart of any city. Some Suburban office spaces are also out there which include midrise structures. They typically range from 80,000 - 400,000 sq ft. Cities also include suburban office parks which have an assembly of such midrise building in a campus-like arrangement.

- **Retail**
  Divided into four kinds, retail commercial estates are everything from small regional shopping centers to huge malls that attract customers from far away.

- **Strip Centers:** These are small retail properties that might or might not have anchor tenants. An anchor tenant is a bigger tenant which draws other customers to the property. Wal-Mart (ASDA in the UK), Home Depot or IKEA are three such examples. Strip centers typically have a mix of smaller retail stores which have various eating outlets, salons or dry cleaners.

- **Power Centers:** Power centers as compared to strip centers have several small retail stores as compared to strip centers but are distinguished by a handful of major retailers such as, Wal-Mart, Staples and Best Buy etc.

- **Out Parcels:** Majority of the large retailers contain more than one out parcels. These are larger chunks of land which are set aside for individual tenants such as banks or local fast food restaurants.

- **Regional Malls:** These include malls which range from 400,000 – 2,000,000 sq ft. A handful of anchor tenants and departmental stores are included in these.

> **Multi-Family**
Multifamily estates are also considered one of the biggest types of investment in commercial real estate sector. These residents include apartments which may vary by location and are usually from garden, midrise to high-rise apartment complexes. They are situated both in urban and suburban areas. The leases here are usually of a shorter-term (1 to 2 years). These apartment buildings facilitate more than one family and contain multiple units which range from 10-100+ units with elevators.

> **Hotels**
These include hotels which provide customers from limited to full services and are located in business districts or famous tourist spots. There are also some extended service hotels which have larger rooms with kitchens designed for families who plan to stay more than a week.
Keep in mind however, that making investments in hotels should come after you have earned enough to play big. This sort of investment is not for beginners. On the brighter side, if you have someone whom you can build a team with—go ahead and invest in this venture.
Hotel real estate investors also get a list of perks. For example, free personal usage along with the occupancy of superior rooms.

Things to remember when looking for a commercial real estate deal

> **If set on commercial estates, be prepared to start low**
> Being on the safe side is always better—those big moves can take time to come around. No matter how much knowledge you have of real estate, you must be prepared for the fact that your investments may take time. So enter only if you are fully equipped to fight the storms.

> **Talk with commercial other real estate investors**
> It will never hurt if you talk with those who have already steered their ships deep in the commercial estate investment businesses. See if they can provide you with tips that can help you gain expertise in the local market.

- **If you are a start up real estate investor, look somewhere else**
  If you are not starting from solid financial grounds and long experience in the real estate sector, you should not enter the commercial world. Since beginners get confused easily, you should first focus on other ways to invest.

- **Remember, it's all about how you handle your business relationships**
  A commercial estate builds on good relations with clients and customers. The more you build a strong base, the further you will grow financially.

- **Remember, commercial investments have longer leases**
  Unlike residential leases, commercial leases run for a longer period of time ranging from 1 to 5 years. Longer lease can also run till ten years or way more.

- **Learn how to negotiate with the potential tenants**
  Commercial estates return a healthy cash flow when managed effectively. Lenders are advised to negotiate at their absolute best in order to attract and keep tenants.

- **Create a balance between rentals and vacancies**
  Depending on your position you should learn to strike a good balance between minimizing vacancies and maximizing rents. I know of one property in Manchester in the United Kingdom

that was vacant for about 2 years because the rental threshold was too high. It's only after the landlord reduced his rental price that a tenant moved in shortly after. It's not wise to refuse a low monthly rent and to be stubbornly set on keeping your property empty.

> **Be sure that you can stand the risk involved**
Although commercial investors have a good chance to pocket consistent cash flows, they must understand that there might be periods where their property will be sitting vacant for many months.

Finding and holding on to a deal of commercial real estate is not just about settling on a good price or picking the right property—its core goes back to handling basic human to human communication so well that you are able to handle sellers and buyers both.

Passive Real Estate Investment (REIT)
Producing a passive income is a type of real estate investment which will help you if you don't feel like being active or involved in the investments. In a nutshell, passive investments are those which provide you cash flows without you putting in any efforts. You make money whilst you sleep!

If this sounds like you then have a look at these kinds of passive investment strategies

> **Real Estate Investment Trusts, REITs**
Simply put, REIT stands for Real Estate Investments Trusts which consists of a real estate property which has mutual funding and multiple stocks. Here, a good number of people create a pool of their combined investments and form a trust. They then allow the REIT to purchase heavy real estate investments such as shopping or apartment complexes etc.

The profit that is produced gets distributed to each individual investor later on. This is one approach in which you can easily get a hands-off opportunity in investments. An advantage of REITs is that these pay 90% of their taxable incomes to investors as dividends. I have helped many people realize their dreams through REITs when they did not have a lot of money of their own individually to make the right kind of investment.

> **Peer to peer lenders**
The P2P lending is pretty old and is still active today. Investors, who have the time and energy to put in real estate, ask other lenders to add passive income which helps them in their portfolio. This type of lending is also a good way to become an investor passively.

Where profits are concerned, peer to peer lending turns out to be healthy, especially for those investors who have more money in their hands and hence, allow higher risk taking.

> **Real Estate Crowd funding**

A crowd funding is a portal of real estate which brings together a pool of investors and sponsors together. The investors have total control over their investments and can invest as little as $5000 on specific funds. This does not need an investor to pitch large amounts of money and also has the path of being actively involved in real estate wide open for those who want to.

> **Tax Liens**
> You can also get your hands on property that has unpaid property taxes. This type of passive investment is known as tax liens sales. In this strategy, investors buy tax lien certificates at   auctions and can also produce healthy returns.

Getting Deeds
Another way to invest in real estate is by getting deeds. A deed is a legal term which transfers some property rights of real estate. Simply explained, this kind of investing is about taking the existing debt of an investor who is unable to pay debts.

Getting deeds can be an advantage since you are not involved directly in credit and are hence not assuming the loan.

> **Types of property deeds**
> The most common type of property deeds are as follows:

Warranty deeds
These deeds transfer ownerships and provide extra benefits as well. The property is free of tax liens and any sort of ownership claims. The transferring party compensates the new owners well if any sort of benefit turns out to be fraud. Warranty deeds are often used for residential sales.

Quitclaim deeds
This deed transfers all ownership rights to the new party. Almost all deeds are carried out in the form of writing and they have no guarantee involved on the extent of the person's interest.

Grant deeds
These deeds transfer interests in a property to the buyer for a price which is agreed upon by both parties. This guarantees that the seller is now the owner of the property and can sell it

legally free of debt. However, it does not give guarantee against any defects of the title.

Bargain or Sale Deeds
Used normally for residential sales, it transfers ownership but does not guarantee that the seller had owned the property free and clear. This deeds resembles a quit claim deed but the property involved here is sold rather than being relinquished.

Flippers vs. Keepers
Investing in real estate is remarkably flexible, no matter what real estate strategy you choose. While this business can go from boom to buzz for a short period of time, there are no chances of it vanishing completely. There is always going to be more things to build and more houses to flip—more properties to let and so on.

Due to this motivation, everybody is seemingly desperate to enter the real estate investing game— either as a flipper or a keeper. If you are confused as to how you want to start your engine, don't worry.

For your ease, I have explained both strategies to show how both of them function. Observe both of these closely and remember to gauge each comparison smartly. Whether you want to be a property flipper or a property keeper depends on your interest and financial objectives.

Keepers are simply those old school real estate practitioners who buy property with the intention of keeping it for a regular cash flow. On the other hand, flippers buy any property with the intention of selling it for a good profit. Both of them have their own pros and cons, and being neither of them is considered good or bad. It all boils down to your investment or financial needs.

Real Estate Flippers	Real Estate Keepers
Real estate flippers invest their money in a certain property for a gain of quick profit which occurs when they fix and sell it.	Real estate keepers like to keep their assets for several years, they are looking for a recurring income from their property.
They invest their time and money on a property for a certain number of weeks or months and like to gain the highest amount of capital appreciation in the shortest time possible.	They want to keep the property so that it slowly reaps financial benefits and also gets appreciated with the passage of time in terms of value.
Flippers do not want the hassle that comes with tenants and cannot afford to manage properties for long periods of time.	Keepers are keen on property management and like to interact with their tenants.
Short term investors.	Long term investors.
They look for properties which require inexpensive fixes rather than major changes.	Keepers look for properties that can fetch high rental incomes.
Do not have large amounts of cash in their hands and hence cannot afford to hold on to a property.	Since they have free cash flow available, they like to maintain multiple properties at the same time.

In a nutshell, whichever strategy you choose to invest in, will depend on your situation. In this digital era, several companies have large amounts of capital available. They want to be on the fast track and hence prefer the flipper intellect. The business managers, who are conservative by nature, tend to avoid risk and remain content with the slow growth rates and cash flows.

However, if you feel like trying both, there is no harm in that as well; since there are people who have made their mark in both of these camps successfully.

Active vs. Passive Investors

So far in this chapter, you have learned about the art of investing in real estate either actively, or passively. Here's the major difference:

To wrap up this part on investment strategies, I strongly recommend that you look before you leap in any of the above investments.

The real question that you should ask yourself now is whether you will be able to pay the price of and manage your investment or not.

Keep a focus on your financial objectives and know how much time you will be able to spare for this activity.

Active Investors	Passive Investors
These investors are actively investing in real estate, thinking of it as a full-time business opportunity.	These investors tend to be passive in their investments and use opportunities as a side business.
Purchase properties for rental incomes or invest their money in fix and flips for gains.	Invest in real estate through mutual funds and investment trusts (REITs).
They are involved in every part of their deal.	Someone else is managing their investments.
The main advantage of active investments is the control they provide, in selection of deals and obtaining finances.	The advantage of passive investment is that you are at a distance and do not have to participate in decision making.
Active investing requires a particularly large sized investment.	Some passive investments can be as low as $5,000.
Types of active investments in real estate: 1. Flipping 2. Buy and hold 3. Airbnb Investments 4. Vacation Rentals	Types of passive investments in real estate: 1. Crowd funding 2. REITs 3. Deeds 4. Tax Liens

How Do I Get Started?

For starters, there are a couple of things you might like to keep an eye on, and are listed below.

Steps towards getting started in real estate investments

1. **Check your finances**

   This starting step is as simple as jotting down all the assets that you own. They might include your various incomes and expenses which get deducted. These finances will help in giving you an idea about how much cash you have for investing. If you have a fine employment record with a good credit score, you won't have any difficulties in getting major loans.

2. **Set your primary and secondary goals**

   So, where do you want to go with your investment? What will it help you to achieve? Are you going for the active or the passive investment? What will you do after you reach your goal? What kind of risks can you bear along the way? All of these questions and some others will help you put down your primary and secondary goals which will help you in staying focused and motivated.

3. **Create a real estate investing business plan**

   Budgeting and creating an investment plan is the only way that you will be able to balance your income and expenses in the real estate sector.

   There are numerous budgeting and planning software available that you can use for productively creating a business investment plan—yes, you got it right, a "business" plan, since real estate is after all a business venture, which earns you profit.

4. Don't wait for it, start sooner
You have read so many books and articles on real estate investments; you have been religiously pursuing various estate agents and lenders for tips on gaining quick wealth, yet when the real deal comes, you come to a halt.

You have to start somewhere and it's better to start simple. If you keep on waiting for the right time, the right property, it probably might not come at all.

5. Get to know your area well enough
It will never be too late to start looking around at properties which are near your location. Get to learn about your neighborhood and not only that, gauge the various buyers and sellers to gain expertise in the art of making investment deals.

6. Don't be quick to sell just yet
When we are enthusiastic, we tend to quickly want to sell our assets in the hopes of making huge returns. This is the worst thing that you can do in some areas of the U.S. or the U.K. In some markets, the longer you wait to sell your property—the better. So again, do your homework find out what works in your particular area.

Top cities in U.S. for making real estate investments 2015

Whichever type of real estate strategy you're trying to invest in, keep in mind the following top five cities located in the United States. These are the top locations which currently offer big cash returns in the real estate market. Location is everything in real estate it determines both rental and asset value.

> **Austin, Texas**
> **Provo, Utah**
> **Houston, Texas**
> **Orlando, Florida**
> **Dallas, Texas**

Chapter 4:

No Money? How to move from Broke to Millions with no money down

Many people have what it takes to be investing and making big returns but unfortunately, they are held back due to lack of funds. Investing in real estate without money may sound too good to be true, but as a matter of fact, it is possible to earn in the estate market without using any of "your own" money. Let's see how.

Can You Invest In Real Estate Without Any Money?

To be honest, the answer to this frequently asked question is, YES, you can! There are multiple ways to do this smartly. However, there IS money involved in every real estate investment and transaction although it doesn't have to be your money.

Let me repeat, the thing to note is that, this money doesn't necessarily have to be coming out of your pocket. Hence you're not investing "without any money" but instead, "without any of *your own money.*" Many people who don't have their own money use "OPM" (Other People's Money) to get their toes wet in the real estate market. OPM is a risk free way to enter the real estate market. Among others, here are some of the ways with which you can invest in real estate with no money down.

Ways to Earn in Real Estate without Money

Let's have a look at the ways in which you can thrive in the real estate market without money.

Before I get to tell you how you can do it without money let me show you how I made millions of US$ in South Africa with only $1000.

I saw an advert of a development that was underway and went to enquire the prices, and to my shock the apartments off plan were for sale for $23000 each with a twelve-month payment plan. The build time was set at 7 months, meaning they anticipated to have completed the building phase of the off plan apartments within seven months, that excited me because I could search for ways to find the remaining $22000 and be able to pay off my apartment even before the anticipated finishing time and even if I failed I knew I still had my twelve month payment plan in place.

I went ahead and paid my deposit of $1000 to hold the property for twelve months and walked away with a guarantee that the price was not to move an inch for the twelve months. To my surprise within 5 months I received a call informing me that the project was finished ahead of time but I still had my twelve-month payment plan intact. Couldn't have been more excited.

I then enquired on how many more apartments were still up for sale and they were sold out. They also informed me that I had made a good decision tying the apartment because the value of the finished product was now $44000. I was ecstatic in a matter of less than 6 months my investment had accrued nearly 50% equity and this figure was set to rise. Right there and then I got a eureka moment. I told the manager there that if anyone wanted my apartment I was selling at $37000 and he told me to call the following morning. I called and lo and behold he had a buyer with him. He bought the apartment for $37500 and I took the $22000 off that price and paid the housing development company and made a cool $15500 from which I took $5500 as income and invested the other 10 000 into the housing developer's upcoming project. 10 off plan apartments to be exact. You see I repeated the same strategy just now I had 10 apartments off plan them moved to 30 off plans doing the same and to other developments until I made millions and until developers I was using realized what I was doing.

I made millions using just $1000 and you can too if you do it right and also learn to shut your mouth on the intentions you have. One of my biggest principles is not to be too much of a talker especially when it comes to investments you're eyeing. Not all people around you are to be trusted.

Lease Options
An option of investing in real estate if you have no money is to go for the lease option. This method includes transferring the control of the property without taking the title. This method is applied on houses of all price ranges. Lease options are a great way to start investing without having to deal with loans or mortgages.

Many people call this process a **"lease option sandwich."**

Let us make it easier for you with the help of this example.

There is an investor who offers a tenant, X, an option of lease on his own property. In the lease paperwork, it's specified that tenant X has a certain period of time; say three years to buy the property for $200,000. Within this time, X pays rent and tries to obtain house mortgage from a bank as well, in order to pay the rest of the amount. So during this time, the investor does not have the allowance to sell his property to someone else because tenant X has the "option" to buy it.

What is a lease option sandwich?
In the lease sandwich, the same process works but with a little curve—the property isn't owned by the investor. In this case, the investor finds this property from a seller and signs a lease option to buy the property for $100,000. The investor then goes out and makes a deal with tenant X for a lease option of a time period lesser than his actual lease. He also charges tenant X a higher amount and gets him to pay $150,000 with bigger monthly rents. So all in all, the investor simply acts as a middle man and ends up collecting the extra $50,000 from this whole arrangement.

People reap big profits without completely owning properties or assets in this way. They do not pay any closing costs and they also have the benefit of cutting back all the cost repairs.

The lease option is a great way for investing in real estate without any risk. But, you have to be sure to enter such a deal with proper research since it can be complicated for beginners.

Tips for using lease options

1. **Try to document everything:**
   A written record for everything that is being agreed upon is always the safe route to choose. Avoid using words like "credit, seller or buyer", instead use terms like, "landlord and tenant."

2. **Consult with an attorney:**
   While drawing up a legal document, it should be kept in mind to consult an attorney who specializes in buying or selling homes.

3. **Keep shorter terms:**
   Set the lease option for a shorter term, for instance a year. If you're a landlord and your tenant wants multiple years for the option, throw in rights to renew the yearly term that you agreed upon. This is because the longer a term is, the more chances it has of being considered as a mortgage by a court.

4. **Always take security deposits:**
   Make it a point to always take security deposits from all tenants.

5. Offer fair prices and reasonable monthly rents:

You have to be fair in your dealing by offering the tenants market compatible rates. Also, make sure you're offering low monthly rents, since the court views them as building equity.

Real Estate Wholesaling

Real estate wholesaling is a process which allows you to get your hands on amazing deals. It's a popular way to jump into real estate investing.

How does Wholesaling function?

To put it in the simplest of ways, a wholesaler is someone who gets paid to find great deals. A person who is wholesaling puts a property under contract and resells it to another investor. They are middle men who acquire a deal and sell that contract for an assignment fee to another retail buyer.

> **The basics of wholesaling in real estate**
A wholesaler normally hardly ever buys any property. They put various properties under contracts and try to quickly sell them for more money. Even if they fail to find someone to buy the property, they walk away prior to the closing of the contract.

Basically, a wholesaler is a middle man—a very well paid one. There are no rehab costs involved, no loan fees, and no hustle with tenants. This is a method which is widely loved by all real estate gurus, and often ends up receiving the most results.

> **The benefits of wholesaling**

1. **No direct money involved:** The top benefit of this process is that you need very little money to do this. All that you will need is loads of ambition and a specialized set of skills in the property market.

2. **No obligation to own property:** Another benefit is that you don't have to be obliged to own the property you are trying to resell. You can always walk away if the deal doesn't fit your requirements. There are many investors who love wholesalers as they have cash in their hands and they are glad to pay it, for getting their hands on the property they want in a short period of time.

3. **No license required:** Being a wholesaler, you will not require any real estate license or work permit. Many wholesalers get paid within days after closing their deals because the buyer that they find usually pays them in hard money or cash.

4. **Anyone can be a wholesaler:** This is a real estate strategy that almost anyone could use—even people with $0 in their hands. You just need a have a strong set of marketing and selling skills along with a growing knowledge of the properties near your location.

> **Tips for real estate wholesalers**

1. **Make it easy for people:**
   If you're a real estate wholesaler, you must have several deals in your consideration if you want to earn quick money. But if you assume that buyers will try to negotiate with you and then buy the contract, then you're making the wholesaling process way too long and risky. Try to make things easier and offer your bottom line up front.

2. **Make it easy for people: Don't count on closing every deal:**
   Unfortunately, in this technique, you don't happen to close every deal you make. In fact, you will see countless deals which will collapse at the closing table in front of your own eyes. So be wary of spending any

amount of the deal's payment before its closing.

3. **Make it easy for people: Don't forget to collect money deposits:**
   Being the middle man, you don't have to feel ashamed to collect your compensation from the buyers. It's very easy for people to back out of deals unless they have paid a non-refundable fee. Its nothing personal and you are in business to make money.

Flips without Funding

This is also a way to start investing using the flipping method. Normally, flipping requires a lot of money. First, you have to buy a house and then pay for its repairs and other maintenance related expenses.

However, there is a certain way to flip a property without using your own cash. This requires you to take money in form of a loan from any source—a private lender, an investment partner or a bank loan.

How to flip houses with no money?

- To flip without any funds, you have to be a champion at providing **"sweat equity"** which is the value of work you put in with the help of your own labor.
- If you are sure that you can give the required amount of time working on the house to flip, then spending this time could turn out to be very lucrative.
- The first thing that you should do is evaluate all your financials and calculate the amount of risk you can take in property flipping.
- Know your credit score since you will need a good score to qualify for a loan. Even if you are taking a private lender, you will have to demonstrate that you will be able to pay your loans with interest. In general, your credit score must hang anywhere between the score of 300-850.
- If your credit score is not good, take some time out to build it before investing. The better your score, the better your house will flip. So, pay all your debts in an efficient manner and build a good record of the loan history.
- In order to flip a house using a loan successfully, you will have to conduct solid background research. Before you begin, it's wise to have a concrete business plan in your hands.
- Keep an eye on the purchases and nearby neighborhoods. Keep a list of expenses which you can afford during the repairing phase.

- Next, you would want to locate a partner who has cash but isn't in the favor of doing the legwork involved. While entering a partnership, you might want to consult an attorney before you sign the deal.
- Have a strong sense of who your potential target buyer will turn out to be. Your flipping will largely depend on whether it's a single family home or a multi family complex.
- You can also use hard money loans to flip houses or go for private money lenders. Hard money however, will not leave you much room for profit.

Private/Hard Money Investing

A well known method for investing in real estate without cash is by using **"hard money"** or **"private money."**

Hard money loans act as a tool for real estate flippers who want to flip a property after fixing it. If you have a killer deal which no one can refuse, you will easily get a hard money loan which will help you in increasing the ARV "After Repair Value" of the property.

Unlike bank loans, these do not depend upon your credit score. Instead, lenders are private and wealthy business owners who provide you a quick short term loan.

However, private lenders usually never care about the investment details and leave it up to you to make all the decisions. They simply want their profit based on the amount they lend. On the other hand, hard money is an arrangement where the lender has a say in where and how their money is going to be used.

Private vs. Hard Money

Both hard and private money are ways to get a loan which excludes the hassle of going to banks and keeping good credit scores. They are quick to get and the terms on the deal could be flexible as the lenders are people who have loads of excess cash to invest. You can negotiate on the payments, repayments and schedule accordingly.

However, if we compare the two loan methods, hard money investors pay a fat price for borrowing according to their convenience, whereas, private lenders can be talked into offering low interest rates to investors and they will be able to keep their profits without needing to split with anyone.

If you are an individual who likes to have total control over their investment, you should work with a private lender. On the contrary, if you like to go by the rules of

your money lender, you can opt for gaining a hard money loan.

Earning through Personal Assets

If you're someone who is young and cannot buy multiple properties or invest in multiple assets at the same time, then this option might be the one where you can kick start earning through real estate.

If you have enough money to just buy or lease your own home to live in it—maybe you should give a thought to turning your very property into an investment.

Most people wait until they have their own properties to invest in secondary ones, while many who want to make quick money, start sooner this way.

Advantages of turning your home into an investment property

The benefits of turning your home into an investment are:

> Being the landlord that lives with the tenant, you get to keep a close eye on all your rentals.
> If your family is small and you have an empty nest, you can easily find multiple young tenants and divide the space among them.
> The cash flow is enough, even if it's coming from a single room, since there are many tenants, especially students who are out there looking for single quarters to pay for.
> If you don't own this property of yours already, these rentals can help you with the lease payments.

Partnerships in Real Estate

A healthy way to invest in real estate if you do not have much capital at hand is through partnerships. Real estate partnerships are very common forms of investments. The reason being, no one can be completely perfect, everyone has something they might lack.

If you think you are a good team leader, you enjoy working with partners and don't dislike dividing your profits—you must consider entering a partnership investment.

For some people however, there can be some cons of making real estate partners that you must be aware of before you make a decision. Therefore, you should look at the following pros and cons of partnerships. After seeing these, depending upon your situation, you can analyze and make an informed decision whether or not you can function in the estate market with a partner.

Pros	Cons
You can get a sizeable pool of resources if you get a good real estate partnership working.	When you grow your team of investors, you are also, by default, dividing your profits.
Two people thinking and coming up with decisions is better than a single person calling the shots all by themselves.	Where there is more than one head involved, differences of opinion are inevitable. Sometimes, you are forced to compromise.
Every investor partner has their own qualities and ways to analyze things. This turns out as a good option where each person fills the gaps that the other left behind.	During the phase of investing with partners, it's often seen that people encounter trust issues and suspicious feelings.
With partners, your tasks and responsibilities are divided—you are able to run the venture without feeling pressured or exhausted.	If you are entering a partnership with someone who is a close friend of yours, chances are that your relationship will end as soon as you will enter a similar business arrangement.
If all partners do their part of the work equally, all of them will be accountable for each action and the risk taken. When one is facing a certain hurdle, the others are also assisting them along the way.	When investing with others, you are indirectly relying on them for your success. Hence, you are bound to get some unrealistic expectations involved.

Things to remember when making partnership investments

> When you're investing with a partner, and you also don't happen to have the bigger amount of money involved as compared to your partner, please understand that you have to be fair while splitting the profits.

> Don't get irritated by all the small details. Like every relationship, you and your investment partner will have to ultimately sacrifice in one way or the other.

> Remember it's a business you are in it for the money you don't have to take that partner home with you so do what you need to and make the best investment decisions.

> Partnership is just like a marriage—don't enter one unless you're prepared to face all that it brings to the table.

> Learn the importance of connecting and networking on a daily basis. Talk every day if possible. Discuss the daily goals and get to know exactly what your partner is working on at the moment.

> Try to plan ahead of time—set up task divisions and define each other's roles and responsibilities in detail.

> Don't avoid the things that give you trouble, ignoring problem areas will not make them go away, discuss them well with your partner and understand/analyze the various risks involved.

- ➤ Choose someone whom you can trust. Try to keep all the partnership agreements on paper for record, just in case you need to show them in the near future.

- ➤ Remember, when you have nothing to lose, half a loaf of bread is better than none. Instead of waiting to save money and then investing, you can explore this strategy to build capital.

Using No Down Payment Loans

While you set out to look for strategies to invest in real estate without any of your own money, you also have the opportunity of using **"no down payment loans."**

There are two major types of no down payment loans: **"VA"** and **"USDA."** Both are a fantastic option for people who want to invest in real estate with no money down. Unfortunately, they are often over-looked by people not having enough experience.

There are a couple of similarities in both VA and USDA loans. The top similarity among them is that they both offer investors 100% financing. Then, there is also the fact that both loans are specific when it comes to the eligibility factor. There is the option of having a flexible

credit score as well. But, of course, some minimum credit conditions do apply.

In some of such loans, a certain amount of fee is charged as a guarantee. For instance, in USDA loans, a fee of 3.5% is charged. But this can be wrapped up along with the loan balance. While most such programs completely eliminate the down payments, some also offer interest-free loans as well.

To help you understand both of them better, below is a list which is comparing USDA and VA loans.

USDA Loans	VA Loans
These are determined by United States Department of Agriculture (USDA).	These are determined by the United State's Department of Veteran Affairs (VA).
These loans are offered to families living in rural areas of the U.S.	These loans were introduced after the World War 2, and are offered to eligible veterans of the U.S.
Their mission is to help the households with lower incomes to obtain reasonable loans.	These loans are offered for the purchasing or refinancing of a primary residence.
Benefits of USDA ➤ 100% financing ➤ No monthly mortgage insurance ➤ No asset requirements ➤ Closing cost gifts allowed ➤ Property improvements are financed into the loan	Benefits of a VA ➤ No or little down payments ➤ No monthly mortgage insurance ➤ Competitive mortgages ➤ Counseling is also provided to some veterans who are facing various financial troubles

To find out about the best loan program which suits you, search your options according to the state you live in, at the **"National Council of State Housing Agencies"** website.

Remember, whichever country you are reading this book from, take time to check what is available in your country. Do not make the mistake of just asking your colleagues, friends or family. Go to a financial institution and get educated.

Where to locate cash for Real Estate?

Even though you don't want to pay for investments, you must however, keep in mind that there will be moments when you'll have to take out your wallet and pay for the bits here and there. Renovations might come your way or simply, you will be required to show cash for the purpose of closing the deal at hand.

In case if you encounter a moment of where you don't have any money left for investing, you can find cash from some of these following places.

1. Friends and Family

This source is one which is very famous and the bright side is that you can always, without hesitation, borrow money for real estate investment from this reliable source. Although this source is easily approachable, it's not as easy as it might appear to be. Doing this sometimes results in spoiling your relationships—so be very careful. In fact, you will be good to go if you consider your friends and family as **"private money lenders"** who are letting you borrow their money and invest it.

As long as you pay your friends or family back, your Thanksgiving dinners won't turn out to be bitter evenings, full of uncomfortable resentments.

2. Banks

One of most widely used source of receiving loan money is a bank. Banks these days are normally pretty laid back and easy on real estate investors. Additionally, as discussed in the previous pages, there are a number of lease options available for you to start earning money by investing.

3. Getting a partner who is willing to invest

This is also a source which was discussed in detail. If you're a good team worker, and you consider yourself as the type of a person who wants to create a perfect partnership, then using this option will surely turn out to be great for you.

If you prove that you have loads of intuition, knowledge and skills, but you lack one thing—financial resources—you will be the person an investing partner will opt for. Oftentimes, partners are those who have more money in their hands but less time to spend it. It's up to you to use this opportunity to place all that you will offer and all that you would require in writing and go ahead with the deal.

4. Mortgage/
Real estate Brokers

You might previously have heard the ideas of using **"real estate or mortgage brokers"** in real estate investments.

A broker is simply a middleman who leads you towards someone who is willing to provide an investment loan. This option is available for people who want quick money and do not have the time to go looking for potential lenders.

Look for real estate brokers who are licensed and well-reputed in their field. They will efficiently do all the legwork for you. For instance, they will be using your credit history and other information to apply for loans for your sake. Some banks have established relationships with your real estate broker and hence, you get qualified for loans without any hassle.

5. Private or Hard Money Lenders

There are thousands of private lenders in the U.S. Also a few exist in the U.K. and also some countries in Africa. These are people who have excess cash in their pockets and are looking for solid investments. You can use either private or hard money lenders, depending on your choice of options. Many investors are more than happy to provide private lenders a 12-20% of a profit return, since they run a real estate investment which allows them to be in full control.

This option is often the one which creates a true win-win situation on behalf of both investors.

6. Credit Cards

One can easily use their own credit card to obtain a large reserve of cash. This can be a solution which will keep you from borrowing money from an outside source. The only thing that might cause you to worry is that you will be paying a good margin of interest for using the credit loan money for real estate investment.

7. Using your home equity

If you have a property which you own, you can easily avail home equity loans. These types of loans can eliminate or deduct interest rates as well. Using home equity loans, owners can take up to $100,000 and yet deduct the total interest during the filing of tax returns.

Things you should remember about home equity

On the other hand, if you are not sure that you are a responsible borrower, you might want to avoid a home equity. They provide huge benefits for lenders as they get to keep the entire amount earned on the initial mortgage.

Many people also make the mistake of falling into the perpetual cycle of spending and borrowing. This turns out to be basically taking a new loan in order to pay for an existing loan or debt. Hence, it's important to take a deeper look at your finances when you decide to borrow against your home.

8. Selling a Part of Your Property

If you have a big nest, think about ways in which you can earn money in the real estate market if you sell some portion of it to invest the cash in another real estate strategy.

9. Borrowing against life insurance

If you have continuously been making life insurance payments on a "cash value" insurance policy, you will have made a considerable reserve amount.

What you can do is borrow this money at a low rate of interest. At the same time, keep in mind that you will be paid a reduced amount of money if you borrow against your life insurance.

10. Getting Personal Loans from Banks

Use a good credit score to negotiate an investment loan from your local bank. Remember, this is a loan and has to be paid back, so calculate your monthly expenditures prior to signing up for any personal bank loan.

11. Selling an Existing Mortgage

Selling of an existing mortgage is something which is fairly common these days. A typical house mortgage is run for a period of 10 to 15 years. During this long period, homeowners are seen to be repeatedly selling their homes before they completely pay their loans off.

This process is simple—you sell the existing property to get money for easily paying off your loan. There are some buyers who eagerly look forward to buying mortgages which have low interest rates.

But before you set out to sell your property and invest in a new one, make sure you are aware of the debt and income ratio of the new investment or property.

12. Using a Combination of The Above

Last but not the least; you can also use a clever combination of the above scenarios.

For example: Investors sometimes use a private money lender for purchasing properties, and then go ahead with forming a partnership investment. Or perhaps they can gather a pool of finances by collecting their life insurance and sell parts of the property they already own when the real estate market is offering high rates.

So, yes, these are some ways in which you can bag money for investments without a lot of sacrifices. Now that you know all these inside secrets and hacks, you possibly cannot use the excuse that says **"I'm too broke for investing in real estate."**

Owner Financing

You can also use owner finance, which is a process by which a property buyer finances the purchase directly through the person or entity selling it. This often occurs when the prospective buyer cannot obtain funding through a conventional mortgage lender, or is unwilling to pay the prevailing market interest rates. The seller may agree to owner financing if he or she is having difficulty selling the property.

Although Owner financing may only cover part of the purchase price, with a smaller bank loan making up the difference, the seller might accept you with no deposit, however he will up the interest rate so as to curb the issue of not having a deposit. This owner finance is also known as "creative financing" or "seller financing".

Understanding Owner Financing

Owner financing is common in a buyer's market. In order to protect his or her own interests, the seller may require a higher down payment than a mortgage lender would. Down payments of 20% or more are not uncommon in owner financing but as aforementioned you can always opt for the high interest rate without need for the deposit.

Also understand that the deed to the property is usually not transferred to the buyer until all of the payments have been made, but because no institutional lenders are involved, the overall terms of financing are much more negotiable, and can be set up to provide benefits to both the seller and the buyer. The buyer saves on points and closing costs, while the seller can obtain monthly cash flows that provide a better return than fixed-income investments. You can put a tenant in the building and they can literally pay off your owner finance!

Chapter 5

Success Tips and Final Words

In this book, I shared with you the various ways by which you can invest money in real estate. Not only that, I also shared numerous ways which you can use if you have no money at all. Now, I want to guide you towards action by providing some success tips and winning secrets along with the final words.

Real Estate Success Tips

Take a look at some of the most helpful real estate success tips. After reading them, encourage yourself towards taking them under consideration.

Never give up on your dreams—no matter what

The life of a fresh real estate investor is filled with countless highs and numerous lows.

You will be high when you close a deal on a particular property, you will drop to low when the market suddenly hits low towards another closing. No matter where you are, you just have to keep pushing, keep striving towards your goal. Not giving up is the No.1 key to success. So, yes—NEVER give up, EVER. Once you taste success in one project it will push you to get past every challenge that presents itself.

Don't turn out to be a jerk

In the world of real estate, there are constantly occurring circumstances where you're going to be working with colleagues on a day-to-day basis. There

will be eager tenants and vicious landlords (it can be vice versa by the way), not to mention a swarm of real estate agents, middlemen or lenders. Yes, not all of them will understand that you have been working hard for a particular project, but you will certainly have to keep your actions in a regular check.

Just like any relationship, your business relations will thrive upon your business interactions and your attitude. This is not just to warn you against being rude and defensive—but it also to inform you that being a jerk can cost you heavily on your next deal.

Be honest
Well, hopefully, you will not need any probing to understand the importance of being honest in each and every investment. Some of the high-profile real estate workers always follow ethics in order to maintain their standard.

Remember never to go about being the over smart individual who strips people off fair profits. Every town has a lot of such people who have their names blacklisted in the market. Such local investors can never be counted upon for their actions, and nobody wants to do business with them as their word means nothing.

Develop your niche
It's important for you to develop a niche and then focus upon it in order to become a master in whichever strategy you go ahead with. Don't hesitate to take your time for selecting this as finding a comfortable niche is essential to turn yourself into a long-term investor.

Once you master a niche, you can go ahead with other areas of real estate. For some people who become a master investor in one particular niche, combining two or more than two niches also works out pretty well.

Start with baby steps
It's easy to get overwhelmed with so many places to go and so much work to do. All you have to do is take baby steps in achieving your goals bit by bit.

Take care of your cash flow
Before trying to move in real estate as a full time business, you have to be careful to have a healthy cash flow. Keep investing for this, until you achieve a cash flow which is exceeding your income from a regular job.

Building a strong momentum
In real estate, usually it is all about finding a healthy momentum between all your deals and actions. You have to be quick in going out and getting things done.

Once you get going, your "money mountain" will develop in time.

Only deal with motivated buyers and sellers
If your potential buyer or seller is not motivated to sell, you might not want to waste your time in dealing with them in the first place. This is because you will not end up settled for the right price.

People who are not fully interested in selling their property might also have a negative effect on you, since you will begin to feel discouraged yourself after dealing with them.

Always ask for expert advice
When you're in favor of a real estate investment plan and you have all the development strategies laid out in front of you step by step, have your plan reviewed by an expert. Only go for someone who is making more money than you do and is generally available for help when you need them around.

At the same time, know that each investment you will be making is a risk; one which every single person in the real estate market takes in order to earn wealth.

Avoid negative thoughts and people
On your way towards the top, you will encounter people who will try to hammer negativity in your mind. These people will often use their "nothing you do is ever going to work" kind of discouraging weapons to bring you down.

It's likely for you to feel like your plans and dreams are worth nothing but pennies, but don't let that kind of negativity bring you down. As a general rule, not every deal you make should transfer 100% profits in your bank account. Sometimes, walking away with 80% is also not bad. In fact, its excellent when you compare it to the case where you are sitting and waiting for the 100% deal, because before you realize it, even the previous openings will go by.

Stay informed, stay educated
Most people absolutely have no idea how important the real estate investment sector has become lately. Keep yourself informed about the locality you're living in and remember that there are many investors who invest in places and properties which they have never even seen. This is the benefit of the digital world. If you are starting completely new, simply allot some hours each day to your real estate venture. Believe it or not, all you will need is a good computer, a phone, a fax machine and a bank account.

Build a huge network

Like journalism, real estate is an endeavor which requires extremely strong networking skills. Your real estate investment network will be the source which will provide you constant support along with new opportunities.

This network should ideally consist of well established mentors, trusted business partners, a list of clients and members of profitable organizations. Don't worry if you don't have them closer to you for now, all these come with the passage of time and learning experience.

Understand the difference between real estate "business" and "investment"

If you're looking for a full blown money making machine, you should look at real estate market with the eye of a businessman, not an investor. In simpler words, don't remain confused between the concept of a real estate business and a real estate investment.

Admittedly, such entrepreneurs often exist who don't want to make millions, and are happy with making healthy profits. They already have another business on the running and real estate helps them in building them a separate cozy nest.

There are plenty of fish in the sea, have patience

There are thousands of fish in the sea. You might think that a certain investment that comes along your way won't knock at you again but always look at multiple prospects before you decide on selecting any one. You don't have to cross the entire ocean in finding your real estate "Dory," but at least consider other similar "nice" investments and compare the pros and cons of each.

Be good at analyzing your finance situation

You have to be realistic. Being honest and fair to your colleagues and partners doesn't mean that you have to foolishly cut back on your profit margins. Try to analyze each deal and see if its making any profit for all the people involved or not.

Look at other investors and their techniques, see the returns of the previous years and keep an eye on the maintenance records for your own benefit. The most important financial figures you should never miss calculating are:

- Your net income and your expenses
- Cash flow (the net income/debt payments)
- Cap rate (net income/price of the property)
- ROI (Return on Investment)
  (Discussed in chapter 2)
- Total ROI you're making per month/year.

Having good marketing skills

If you have decided to go ahead with the real estate business sector, you will have to build a whole setup for marketing it, online and offline both. These days you will find infinite articles which will provide you marketing strategies for your business.

If you are still thinking that only the classifieds will be enough for locating people you will need, you're doing it wrong. With more and more people turning to the internet for the search of properties up for sale, it's essential to carry out a solid online marketing of your real estate business.

Using this tip will save you loads and loads of time as you will be cutting down your major legwork. From providing virtual tours and giving photographs to the target audience, a lot can be done if an investment or a business is staged online.

Remember a small tip; the most important marketing tool you can use is yourself. You should represent your own individual brand. While other marketing tools may require you to dish out money, this one will simply need you and your enthusiasm alone.

The importance of being creative in the real estate market

What I need to educate you as an investor now, is on the importance of being creative in your real estate investments.

Understand and grasp the possibility that there are above a hundred ways in which you can mix and match the dealing strategies and tips mentioned in this book. One of the many valuable roles you have to play as an investor is by using your ability to surface ways forward even when things do not seem to be revolving in your favor.

The point is, money is everywhere around you, you just have to have the creative eye to go out and be creative in all of your deals.

Are you also falling prey to the analysis paralysis?

It can be effortless to fall prey and get stuck in the spiral universe of an **"Analysis Paralysis."**

Many of you can understand and relate to this phase. This is where you are stuck on researching, planning, analyzing, evaluating or simply doing everything except the one thing that you must do—executing!

Yes, planning is an important step in many investment strategies, but even after all the planning, you feel like you're never ready to take action, you probably never will. It's easy to prefer reading and stop you from risking any money, but billionaires weren't born to get stuck in analysis paralysis.

How to overcome analysis paralysis?

> **Don't look for perfection yet**
> Sometimes, settling on a good enough choice that you have is the best decision that you can possibly make.
>
> All steps have their pros and cons like described in this book, don't let this factor steal your dreams.

➢ **Give yourself a deadline**
Explore your strategy and make a business plan that motivates you and gives you a firm deadline for executing particular tasks. If you don't yourself a deadline, you will always end up giving yourself one excuse after the other.

➢ **Practicing the art of making decisions**
This is an exercise which will positively help you in going fast forward in any money making industry. For starters, try to distinguish between the decisions which need your immediate attention and those which can be made later. Remember, decisiveness is something like the famous author Brian Tracy places it.

DECISIVENESS IS A CHARACTERISTIC OF HIGH-PERFORMING MEN AND WOMEN. ALMOST ANY DECISION IS BETTER THAN NO DECISION AT ALL.

BRIAN TRACY

> **Get rid of your fears**
> Several people come forward with the
> confessions that their fear of making mistakes
> or failure is what keeps holding them back
> down. To fight this thought, remember to dig
> for what you fear most and head out to make it
> right? Is it lack of money? If yes, then maybe
> knowledge can save you.
>
> Besides, some successful people build a
> strong momentum by taking actions or making
> adjustments as they move along.

The secret of creating what I call a "mountain" of money

There are two major boulders which act as the base
when you are building a mountain of money.

One is **time** and the other is **money**. Having one is
more than enough for someone to become a
millionaire without having the total use of the other.

Even if you have no money to invest but have an
existing asset which you can effectively utilize for
investing, you can be the winner. The "time" boulder
will be your friend in this case.

It's important to go along keeping the fact in mind that
with the passage of time, real estate does appreciate.
Not only this, but the exciting fact that it simply HAS
to appreciate.

Saying this, and keeping the human history and
population increases in mind, there is an increasing
amount of inflation all around the world especially in

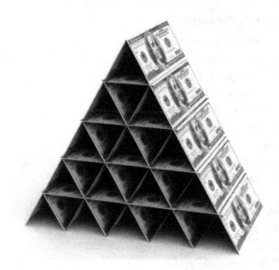

recent times. Not to mention, most countries have a whole history of continued inflation. As afore-mentioned the existence of the land is the same—but there is always an increase in the number of people demanding places for living, working, renting, shopping, and more.

The second boulder "money" is something which even if you don't possess, you can make do without. We have explained in depth about how you can acquire a pool of investment money for real estate.

Okay, we admit that some of the initial investors will still complain about NOT having enough assets to invest. But let's consider the possibility that even you have one brick—that is enough **time** in your hand. You might also be able to understand the logic of money pyramiding, you have nothing to lose, and why can't you start now? What can possibly stop you?

Some Final thoughts

To lay some final words on the table, let's just say that if you want to invest with "no money down" it's not a bad place to start. In fact, thinking that you need lots of money before you will even begin to make profits is wrong. There are hundreds of real estate investors who started from the bottom and they have successfully achieved a higher threshold. Remember, *If you are unable to make money without money, you will fail at making money with money!*

It works on the simple logic that the more you are learning from each deal you finalize, the more you are earning. Of course the start will be slow, but you will get there eventually. All it will take is hard work, knowledge and a place to start with.

This is it; the rest of the money making is entirely up to you. As you start, the small rewards will make it worthwhile and motivate you in reaping the bigger rewards. By the time you are finishing this book, all the pieces will automatically fall together, making you understand the world of real estate investing. Once you have discovered the informational key to making big bucks after reading this, you can keep using this book as a reference manual for getting ideas and making selection of multiple strategies while buying investment properties.

Making you aware of the various investment opportunities in the real estate market is my aim. Now stop reading and get ready to make your million-dollar dream come true by successfully kick starting a profitable real estate business investment. Remember the best investment on earth is earth.

See you at the top.
It's too crowded at the bottom!

CPSIA information can be obtained
at www.ICGtesting.com
Printed in the USA
BVHW010411251118
533785BV00011B/257/P

MODERN
ROME

4 GREAT WALKS
FOR THE CURIOUS TRAVELER

DIANNE BENNETT AND WILLIAM GRAEBNER

CURIOUS TRAVELER PRESS

Cover photo: Entrance to Museo della Civiltà Romana, EUR

info@curioustravelerpress.com

716.353.3288

CONTENTS

PREFACE

Why a New Volume?

OUR FIRST BOOK, *Rome the Second Time: 15 Itineraries That Don't Go to the Coliseum,* as well as our blog—www.romethesecondtime.com—made us long for more. We sat around, sipping a fiano or a falanghina in our favorite wine bars, talking about the walks we didn't include in the book, and the limitations of a blog. How could we have left out Garbatella, we kept asking ourselves, especially the year we lived next door to this fascinating social experiment of a neighborhood? Did we, devotees of 20th-century modernism, really omit (except for brief mention in a Monte Mario itinerary) the *Foro Italico* and all of EUR? And our 2008 sojourn in Flaminio, where we wrote most of *Rome the Second Time,* underscored the appeal of that nascent district that, in just a decade, emerged as modern Rome's cultural center.

And so began the debate—he said/she said—should we update *Rome the Second Time*? Should we publish an entirely new book? And finally the decision to publish three itineraries as a separate eBook only. Three, you say, but there are four! Yes, another debate. After traipsing up and down hidden stairways in Los Angeles, following a trend on the West Coast to do "stairway" walks in the great cities there, we concluded we could do the same for Rome. As do many of our ideas, this one began as an experiment, then was to be a blog post, and finally became the fourth walk in our new eBook, though capturing it under "modern" is a bit of a stretch.

It's now about four years and dozens of walks and drafts later. This small volume took hundreds of hours of work, both at the keyboard and on the streets of Rome, as well as months of research, in English and Italian sources.

Restricting this new, small volume to four itineraries called for restraint. Yes, we left out Tuscolano and Pasolini's beloved Mandrione. Yes, we wanted to incorporate the architecture of 21st-century Roman Catholic churches. Yes, we could have done something special with the city's emerging avant-garde arts community, its intriguing spaces located in Portonaccio, Casaletto, Torpignattara, and Pietralata, among others. There's no limit to Rome's layered wonders.

We'll leave you with a very Italian phrase. The Italians wish everyone *buon* or "good" something, whatever it is. For concerts, *buon ascolto* (good listening); for eating, *buon appetito*; for traveling, *buon viaggio*. And so, to our readers: *buon walking.*

PHOTOS

All photos are by William Graebner and Dianne Bennett.

ACKNOWLEDGMENTS

In *Rome the Second Time,* we thanked the many Rome friends and colleagues who shared with us the wonders of the Eternal City. With this small book, we thank them once again. We add especially for *Modern Rome* our debt to Professor Pia Schneider, Rome Program Resident Director, Iowa State University, who gave us a delightful walking tour of Garbatella, from the perspective of someone who lives there and has taught its architecture and social spaces. We have learned a great deal from Paul Baxa and his recent book, *Roads and Ruins: The Symbolic Landscape of Fascist Rome,* and from Gianni Rivolta's *Garbatella: Tra storia e leggenda.* We thank our readers, the followers of Rome-the-Second-Time's Facebook group and of our blog, www.romethesecondtime.com, whose ideas and comments inspired us to write this new book and helped keep Rome fresh to us. Finally, we reserve never-ending gratitude for our dear friend in Rome, Massimo Vizzaccaro, not only for his gentle correction of everything we say and do that's not quite right—no mean feat—but also for being willing to be the native Roman reader of our efforts, yet one more time. We asked Massimo simply to read the draft for our Italian errors. He did so much more than that, checking our research and, now and then, sharing with us, and ultimately with our readers, the connections between our narrative and the Rome he knows so intimately.

AUTHORS

William Graebner is a widely published author of books on American history, including *Patty's Got a Gun,* about Patricia Hearst. Dianne Bennett was managing partner of Hodgson Russ LLP, Buffalo's largest law firm. When not in Rome, getting around on their Malaguti 250, a large scooter, they live in Buffalo, New York, and Los Angeles, California.

GARBATELLA

Garden City Suburb

Garbatella, AN EARLY 20th-century suburb of Rome, is one of our favorite places. At once monumental and intimate, this sprawling, complex, planned community is unique to the city. It speaks eloquently, and with unparalleled charm and drama, of the political, economic, and social contradictions of the era that began with the end of World War I. More than a monumental housing project (although it certainly was that)

On via della Villa Lucina, one block south of
largo delle Sette Chiese, not on itinerary

1

or a delightful, creatively conceived planned community (although it was that, too), Garbatella was a grand stage on which the tensions of the inter-war years were inscribed, lived and—perhaps most incredibly—preserved for contemporary observers to see and feel.

But it isn't for everyone. Garbatella isn't for shoppers; most of its shops are on its northern border, the business-like boulevard, Circonvallazione Ostiense. And it isn't for those seeking a high-level dining or wine-bar experience. Garbatella *is* for those with an interest in 20th-century architectural and design history, especially the history of urban planning; those curious about the politics and aesthetics of Italian Fascism; those seeking a glimpse of the experience of Rome's inter-war working class; and, perhaps especially, those who savor the allure and mystery created by the hills, curving streets, enchanting stairways, and interior courtyards that define the place called Garbatella.

Perhaps because Garbatella is so real, so starkly authentic—or seems so, anyway—it has produced and attracted a wide range of celebrities and public figures, including novelist Pier Paolo Pasolini, who reveled in the companionship and class contours of its piazzas and bars. The famed actor Alberto Sordi grew up in Garbatella on via Vettor Fausto, and the young protagonist of the social-realist classic *Ladri di Biciclette* (*The Bicycle Thief*) [1948], was living in Garbatella's *Lotto* #9 when he was discovered by Vittorio De Sica. Director Nanni Moretti scootered through Garbatella in his own classic, *Caro Diario* (*Dear Diary*) [1993]. And Gandhi—yes, Gandhi—stopped in Garbatella, specifically at the "white hotel" in Piazza Biffi, during his two-day stay in Rome in December 1931. You'll see most of these locations on this walk.

Favorite son

Garbatella was first called Concordia, apparently to suggest the ideal of diverse social classes existing in harmony—a goal of all western societies experiencing class tensions while undergoing rapid industrialization and urbanization. But that name was fleeting, and Garbatella soon took hold. The new name is said to have originated with a well-mannered (*garbata*) innkeeper (*ostella*), serving food in an *osteria* on via delle Sette Chiese: hence Garba/tella. Others say the key combination derives from *garbata* and *bella*. Those who claim to know think it more likely that Garbatella describes a method of grape cultivation (*a garbata*) once used in the area, but the friendly innkeeper (arguably by the name of Carlotta, according to some sources) continues to be memorialized, as we will see on this itinerary.

Although Garbatella was destined to be mostly a housing area, the first plan for the then-unsettled tracts south of Rome's Pyramid called for something quite different. In the early 20th century, Paolo Orlando, a creative technocrat, broached the idea of turning a two-mile swath (including both Garbatella and what is now Ostiense) into an industrial and commercial area, served by a new river port to be located on the *Tevere* near the Basilica of *San Paolo fuori le Mura* (St. Paul's Without [Outside] the Walls). The port was to be made possible by the digging of a canal across one of the great bends in the river. That never happened, nor did Ostiense become quite the factory hub that Orlando and others envisioned. Nonetheless, there was enough new industrial activity, as well as demand for housing to serve the families streaming into Rome from the countryside or removed from the neighborhoods in Borgo Pio (near the Vatican) and around the city's government center, the *Campidoglio* (Capitoline Hill), to suggest the need for a new community on the small hill to the south of Ostiense: that is, Garbatella.

The project would be undertaken by the *ICP*—the *Istituto per le Case Popolari* (Public Housing Association), created by Ernesto Nathan, Rome's first mayor to come from other than the city's elite, partly in response to public protests over the meager government resources given to housing the city's working-class majority. The land, owned by the Italian Navy, was inexpensive. A bevy of young architects, supervised by Gustavo Giovannoni and eager to innovate and experiment in the difficult task of providing housing for the masses, lent their considerable talents to the project.

The first building block was set in place in 1920, and in less than 15 years a rocky bluff had become a model "suburb," one of the most unusual and compelling communities in the western world.

HOW TO GET THERE

The itinerary proper begins at Piazza Brin, located roughly mid-way between two stops on the Metro B line: Garbatella and Basilica San Paolo. You can reach Piazza Brin from either of these stops, listed below as First Alternate Approach and Second Alternate Approach. The Garbatella Metro stop is the end point of the itinerary. See Walk 1 Itinerary.

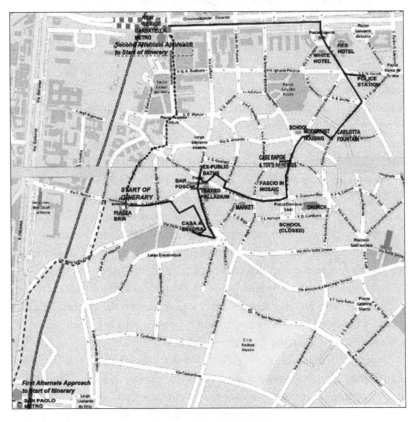

Walk 1 Itinerary

First Alternate Approach to Piazza Brin. From the Basilica San Paolo stop: as you descend the station stairs, exit left to via Ostiense and walk north (right), past the basilica on your left to via delle Sette Chiese (Seven Churches Street), an historic pilgrimage route that curves right, up the hill. Follow this street over the tracks, then take the first left—via Alessandro Cialdi—one long block to the bottom of the stairs below Piazza Benedetto Brin. Ascend the stairs and cross the park. Avoid the park and stairs after dark.

Second Alternate Approach to Piazza Brin: From the Garbatella stop: use the via Pullino exit, look (but don't walk) left; if you've exited properly, you'll see the new Ostiense bridge. At the via Pullino sidewalk ahead, turn right and continue for about 200 yards (meters) to a small piazza, Piazza Augusto Albini,with a circle in the middle. Turn right here and take the first crosswalk left, continuing on via Pullino. At nos. 14–16 on the left, note the elegant modernist mid-century doors, and just beyond at via Pullino no. 1 on the right, a left-wing *circolo* (social organization), downstairs. At the corner ahead, enter Piazza Pantero Pantera (full of parked cars) and follow the road uphill to the right, beneath the sign for the restaurant *L'Isola dei Sardi Due.* Walk uphill on this street, via Alberto Guglielmotti, taking due notice of the street art on your left (at about 30 yards [meters]). It's another 100 yards (meters) to the crest of the hill and Piazza Benedetto Brin. Across the street from the building is a small park, complete with fountain and, toward the river, a nicely designed stairway leading to the street below. In the past, the area was degraded by graffiti and the scene of the occasional drug deal. Avoid the park and stairs after dark.

PIAZZA BRIN

The building that dominates the piazza was not the first to be completed, but it was among the first, and it is the historic entrance to Garbatella. Finished in 1922, it was designed by Innocenzo Sabbatini, by all accounts the most influential of all the architects who had a hand in the area's architecture. Here, Sabbatini offers a balanced façade, but also a richly decorated and eclectic one, with elements and details reflecting several eras of Rome's history: medieval, pre-Renaissance (the arches above the restaurant), and ancient (fragments found during construction were here and there incorporated into the façade). The restaurant on the left side of the building, *Dar Moschino* (Moschino's Place) is excellent and relatively inexpensive, serving authentic Roman cuisine, including tripe and rabbit; reservations recommended.

There are two plaques near the arch, one laid on February 18, 1920 by King Vittorio Emanuele III, celebrating the development of the *ICP* along

Piazza Brin

with the hyped maritime and industrial development. The other was laid in 2010, commemorating the 90th anniversary of Garbatella: "for 90 years the beating . . . heart of Rome. To its children: strength, passion, intelligence in the life of the city."

Walk through the arch (this is public space) to the courtyard beyond and look back at the building. On the left, a sign identifies the *lotto* (block, but for us, an apartment building) of the building (*Lotto* #5) and the group responsible for the project, the *ICP.* The building's colors and its gardens echo the countryside. Building materials recuperate the Italian past: near ground level, the peperino and yellowish tufo suggest the ancient Roman heritage, while the brick/tufo mix higher up evokes the medieval/pre-Renaissance era. The roughly-cut gargoyles at the roof line are vernacular in spirit, a concession to the ordinary people who would inhabit the building and the community.

Continue through the courtyard, as via Luigi Orlando—very much, and intentionally, a "country" lane—curves gently left and crosses a street. This phase of the Garbatella project called for a village of comfortable, charming, but small (650 square feet [60 square meters]) apartments, painted in rural colors—yellows, reds, and ochre—designed to appeal to the residents, who were by and large recent migrants from the countryside.

From the beginning, and perhaps only in the beginning, planners envisioned a neighborhood that resembled the English garden cities of the era (influenced by the socialist Robert Owen), with common vegetable and decorative gardens and featuring small villas (*villini*) with open gates in a rustic *barochetto* (little baroque) style. *Barochetto* was derived from the medieval and philosophically drawn from the anti-capitalist, anti-industrial ideas of William Morris, John Ruskin,

Designed to look as if the water drains through the gargoyle

and the larger Arts and Crafts movement that was especially strong in England and the United States. Garbatella is also kin, though more remotely, to the rigorously planned American "green" cities of Franklin D. Roosevelt's New Deal: Greenbelt, Maryland; Greenhills, Ohio; and Greendale, Wisconsin, all built in the late 1930s.

Not far ahead, at no. 5 on the right, enter the complex and take the path just to the left of the painting on the wall. Beyond, jog left or right around the communal clothes-drying area. At the next building on the right, note the subtle references to the baroque above the center arch and, above left, an example of a possibly illegal (*abusivo*) addition to the structure, that is, one carried out without the permission of the authorities. Continue on to the larger "piazza," with its substantial (and again communal) play area with a stone floor, another sign of the desire of the architects to construct a complex that would enhance and preserve a sense of community among people from different towns and villages.

Take a left at the front of this play area and a right just *before* the fence, following the set of buildings on the left. On the right, note the large glass staircase—a touch of modernism that would be replayed in the hotels built later—and, further on, a nicely planted and well-maintained courtyard.

Communal space

Bear and curve right to the front of the building—the *Casa a Esedra*—the semi-circular complex, located on via delle Sette Chiese (*Lotto* #10). Designed by Angelo Vicario in a style suggesting a patrician palace, the façade features the Fascist numbering system. The date of completion (here, on the façade, 1928) usually can be determined by adding the Roman numeral—here, VII—to the year 1922, when the March on Rome launched the Fascist era. In this case, oddly, the numbers don't work. In any event, the scale and look of this apartment house are very dif-

Classical references in public housing

ferent from the Piazza Brin structure and the country-lane appeal of the earlier buildings.

Carry on down the steps of the *Casa a Esedra* to via delle Sette Chiese, a street designed for pedestrians only, but that now (surprise!) has automobile traffic. Go left, up the street to the piazza at its end. On the right, there's a bar for coffee, water, or a beer. But we would hold off until the next piazza. Curve left and take the first street (via Enrico Cravero) downhill, next to *Lotto* #11. Across the street, another *lotto* features a handsome arched entrance and, above it, the words *"Istituto Per Le Case Popolari"* (Public Housing Association). Atop the building, note the Renaissance-like towers, arches, and columns.

An entrance to a *lotto*

Via Enrico Cravero flows into Piazza Bartolomeo Romano, a special place, even for Garbatella. The impressive building that dominates the piazza is the *Teatro Palladium,* restored and now owned by the Third University of Rome and site of regular talks and cultural programs in music, dance, theater, and art. Designed by Sabbatini and constructed in 1927, it was then a theater and cinema—the only cultural facility in the area. Above the *Palladium* (then known as the Cinema Garbatella) were housing units,

Hip crowd at the *Teatro Palladium* at dusk

occupied in the 1930s by artists. Perhaps the most significant of the many modifications to the building was the enclosing of the front porticoes, giving the structure a somewhat heavier feel than the original.

Across the piazza, you can't miss the patio at *Bar Foschi,* a favorite hangout of young artists and academics, now as in the past. There's usually no table service, so step inside and order a beer, a coffee, or a glass of wine and take it out to the table (no extra charge). Pier Paolo Pasolini now and then enjoyed the sociability of *Bar Foschi,* perhaps while scouting the area for actors for his films and stories for his novels. Some of the young men described in Pasolini's 1959 novel *Una Vita Violenta (A Violent Life)* were from Garbatella.

PUBLIC BATHS

Across the street to the left, as one faces the *Palladium,* is another Sabbatini building (also 1927), the *ex-Bagni Pubblici* (ex-Public Baths), a building made necessary by the scarce bathing facilities in the public housing projects; none of the larger buildings had baths or showers. People would come on a Friday or Saturday for their weekly bath, perhaps taking advan-

Once public baths, now a furniture store

tage, too, of the services of a barber or hairdresser, also located in the building. Today it's a furniture store—*Proietti*—rather than the museum it should be, but the interior still evokes the public bathing era and suggests Sabbatini's debt to the house of Diana at Ostia Antica. Go in. The current owner is well-versed in the building's history and willing to explain it, though his only language is Italian. On the first floor, note the round tiles of glass/cement which allowed the glow of the boilers below to come through. The large arches on the building's façade reference the Baths of Caracalla—a way of educating the common people who bathed here to their ancient heritage.

Like the *Palladium,* the public baths combined services with housing, and behind the building one gets a sense not only of the scale of the Garbatella project, but of how the architects envisioned public space. Exiting the bath building in the direction of the *Palladium,* go around back, into the courtyard. As you walk through to exit toward the back/right, note the strong visual stonework on the corners of the buildings—a Renaissance reference—and the different window treatments, as well as the experiment in asymmetry that characterizes the whole. Here, as in the first large courtyard we saw, the architects labored to create a variety of public spaces—for children's play, for domestic work (drying clothes), for adult socializing—and, unlike many condominiums in Rome—all accessible from several entrances. The public, rather than a *portiere* (doorman), controls this space.

Curve gently right toward the back exit, then bear right at the gate, on via Vettor Fausto (where actor Alberto Sordi grew up). Turn around and glance upward: on the second floor (Italian first), the architect offers a window *à la* Francesco Borromini, a playful exercise in perspective.

RADICAL GARBATELLA

Turn right on via Vettor Fausto, then left in about 25 yards (meters) on via Francesco Passino. Up a short block on the right is Garbatella's newly refurbished market with its unusual rounded façade (the original project was completed only in 1952, the reconstruction in 2012) and, just beyond, two important sites of Garbatella's radical politics. Indeed, for years before the recent reconstruction, the closed market, too, participated in Garbatella's leftist politics; the words "*GARBATELLA ANTIFASCISTA*" (Anti-Fascist Garbatella) appeared in a large painted banner just above the stairways.

The public market before restoration

Garbatella's radicalism has deep roots. Garbatella's hotels, which we'll see later on the itinerary, at times served as detention centers for communists and other leftists deemed dangerous to the Fascist state. And when Hitler made his one and only visit to Rome in 1938, potential dissidents were rounded up and brought to the hotels, where they were placed under police guard. As a result, state policies created a dissatisfied and angry population. Moreover, the great majority of the men living in the new housing in Garbatella were proletarians—poorly paid workers struggling to keep their jobs and feed their families under the difficult conditions of the worldwide Great Depression. These workers were especially vocal, and most likely to incur the wrath and intervention of the police, as May 1—Europe's Labor Day—approached. In late 1943, with Fascism disintegrating and the city occupied by the Nazis, some 270 of the most disaffected—from the working-class neighborhoods of Ostiense, Testaccio, and San Saba, as well as Garbatella—formed a resistance organization with like-minded anti-Fascists. For more on centers of anti-fascism, see RST's post and Paul Baxa's Roads and Ruins: The Symbolic Landscape of Fascist Rome.

Even today Garbatella is known as Rome's most socially progressive neighborhood. In June 2013, during a run-off campaign for Mayor, the incumbent candidate of the conservative, center-right party, Gianni Alemanno, was subject to verbal attacks during a tour of Garbatella. About 40 militants from two leftist social centers in the area—"Acrobat" and "La Strada"—shouted "*vattane a casa*" (go home), "*non ti ci vogliamo qui*" (we don't want you here), "*Alemanno pezzo di merda*" (Alemanno's a piece of s…), and "*fuori i fascisti dalla Garbatella*" (get the fascists out of Garbatella). Some spit on the Mayor's cavalcade. Alemanno was soundly defeated in the general election, not only in Garbatella but in every other section of the city.

The colorful graffiti that covers the building (like the market, built in 1952) at the corner of via Passino and via degli Armatori, at the back of the market, present the area's radicalism in more civil terms, and with more of an international perspective. One piece appears to be dedicated to Islamic women, another quotes from the Cuban revolutionary (Argentine-born) Che Guevara, a third seeks "Freedom and Justice" through breaking the manacles of oppression, and a fourth is about the quest for peace. The center for one of the leftist groups is located just around the corner on via degli Armatori, in a cavernous room below street level. Have a look.

Inside a leftist social center

Across via degli Armatori on via Passino, a community courtyard represents the more prosaic side of Garbatella's politics; here local political groups host events with a social flavor, including food, beer, and music—and of course, speeches that last too long. The small building here is reputed to be the oldest in Garbatella.

THE PLANNED CENTER

At the crest of the hill ahead—the highest point in Garbatella—lies Piazza Damiano Sauli, which the planners intended as the center of the community. An enormous public school (now closed), designed by Angelo Brunetta and completed in 1930, holds forth at one end of the piazza, with its handsome and elaborate cupola in iron and four large Fascist eagles perched on the façade. To the left of the school, a church from the same period, by Alberto Calza Bini, is significant for its enormous dome, visible throughout Garbatella, and for its refined neoclassical interior, reminiscent of Borromini. The piazza was the setting for the first meeting of Tommaso and Irene, the protagonists of the 1962 film, *Una Vita Violenta (Violent Life)*, based on Pasolini's novel.

Fascist-era public school, now closed, on Piazza Sauli

There's one more item of interest in the piazza, and to find it you'll have to turn your back to the school, cross the street at the end of the piazza, and move a few yards (meters) to the left. There, in the sloping art work between the asphalt and the stone sidewalk, a survivor of the Fascist epoch: a *fascio*—the most important of the symbols of Mussolini's regime—perfectly crafted in small black and white stones. Don't miss it!

CASE RAPIDE

Still with your back to the piazza, cross under the arches on via Giovanni Battista Magnaghi.

Along this street, on both sides, you can see the *case rapide* (quickly built homes), identifiable by their rough stucco exteriors: *Lotto*s #20 on the left, then #40 and #44. These houses, built, as their name indicates,

Garbatella loves a street party—via G.B. Magnaghi

quickly, deteriorated quickly as well. The initial plans for Garbatella were for a carefully constructed village. But as the Fascists gained in power and moved more Rome residents out of the center to outlying areas or from the countryside into Rome, the need for immediate hous-

Roma fans decorate deteriorating *case rapide*

ing became pressing. As a result, the more carefully designed and constructed homes gave way to smaller, cheaper, rapidly built homes. The first street on the left, via Vittorio Cuniberti, is full of *case rapide,* and if you walk about 15 yards (meters) down it, you will see on the left a house painted in honor of Rome's most famous soccer player, Francesco Totti, still playing at 36 as of 2013. The yellow and red are his team (Roma) colors. You will find Garbatella full of yellow and red. There are no white and sky-blue signs for Lazio, the competing, right-wing Rome team, in left-wing Garbatella.

AN EDUCATION TEMPLE

Continue along via G. B. Magnaghi to the piazza ahead, Piazza Nicola Longobardi. The piazza and the elementary school that dominates it were designed by Sabbatini, whom we met at Piazza Brin and again as the architect of *Teatro Palladium.* The school, built in 1927–31, is classical in design, a true "temple" to education. Like other public buildings in Garbatella, and in contrast to the residential buildings, it is more formal, more classical, with references to the past. In back, the school creates a courtyard; the Fascists wanted children all'aperto—outside as much as possible. And the upper floor, you will note, is deliberately designed to be more child-sized. Look to your left as you face the school, and you will get another dose of the Roma team's colors.

More Roma fans at work

To the right of the piazza, as you face the school, is a building that reflects pure modernism and rationalism. Although atypical of most Garbatella buildings, it was built in 1931, not late in the community's development. This is *Lotto* #27 out of about 50; the *lotto*s were numbered as they were built. Architect Giuseppe Nicolosi takes advantage of the sloping terrain by using staircases and different levels in the complex. Each

Modernist housing

side of the building has four apartments. Go down the stairs and into the courtyard beyond to get a feel for its balanced rationalism and modernist sensibilities, as well as its deterioration, unfortunately.

Exit to the back right of the complex onto via Roberto de Nobili. Walk left a half block to Piazza Ricoldo da Montecroce. On your right here, at the base of the stairs, informally referred to as "lovers' staircase," is one of the icons of Garbatella, *La Fontana di Carlotta,* or Carlotta's fountain, designed by Sabbatini. The fountain has been providing Garbatella's residents with pure water, and ample opportunities for vandalism, since the mid-1920s.

Continue downhill on via R. de Nobili to the next piazza, Piazza Ceremia Bonomelli. High up on the building at your left is a *bas relief* of the legendary gracious innkeeper who gave the name to the neighborhood and the words, on a ribbon, *La Garbatella*.

THE HOTELS

We are about to move into a very different part of Garbatalla, the hotels. So this is a good time to stop and reflect on the variety of residences and public buildings we have seen in this planned community. There were many innovations here, including the Y style of apartment buildings, providing cross-ventilation, buildings that have different relationships to the streets, buildings that are stepped back to allow more light and air, even apartment bathrooms. These innovations contrast with the older and less well-planned neighborhoods for the working class, such as San Lorenzo. The variety of concepts the young architects brought to the projects here make each spot seem like a movie set, with changing scenography as one moves through the area.

Turn left, to the right of the *La Garbatella* building, on viale Guglielmo Massaia. On your right, on this block, is one of the four massive hotels, and

The "red hotel"

beyond, also on your right, in the next piazza, is the "red hotel" (*Lotto* #42). As noted above, the hotels fomented dissent, in part because they were where dissidents were sent—far from the center of Rome at that time, but not so far from the Ostiense train station where Hitler arrived in 1938. The hotels also housed ex-prisoners returning to Rome after incarceration elsewhere. What were the usually manipulative Fascists thinking?

As initially planned by Sabbatini, the hotels were to have been temporary housing for pilgrims coming to Rome for the 1933 Jubilee Year. In the Catholic religion, a Jubilee year is a year of universal pardon. Usually held every 25 years, this was an extra one commemorating Jesus' death. The "red" and "white" hotels (the white hotel is *Lotto* #41) that face the next piazza, Piazza Eugenio Biffi, had tiny bedrooms and shared bathrooms, cooking facilities, and living rooms. Again, the pressing needs of the great influx of working-class people thrown out of their homes in areas such as Teatro Marcello and Porta Metronia resulted in a change in the hotels to bare-bones housing. Sabbatini apparently resigned rather than modify his original designs.

The hotels were not popular with the residents. They not only resented being forced out of their former neighborhoods, but also disliked having to leave their furniture behind for the iron tables and chairs provided by the complexes. The hotels had cement walls around them, and the residents lived under a regime of "extreme control," as one book on Garbatella puts it.

A sense of design and urban innovation, in addition to history, marks the hotels for our interest. Walk ahead to the piazza (Piazza Michele da Carbonara) and around to the front of the hotel on your right and into the police station in its center. If you are able to go farther inside, you may be able to see the gorgeously-laced dome. Notice also the prominent and distinctive staircases, bringing light to the interior. Return to the piazza around which the four hotels are centered, Piazza M. da Carbonara, and continue on the street you took down from the last piazza, viale G. Massaia, to get the best view of the red hotel. If you look at the top of the red hotel you will see a well-designed clock, with the time stopped; it broke when the Allies in World War II bombed the area. According to legend, the clock remains at that time as a memory of the bombing. The red hotel had a *mensa* or common dining facility in the middle of one of the courtyards. It was destroyed in the bombing by the Allies, who were targeting nearby railroad tracks and industrial facilities in nearby Ostiense. Another hotel had a clinic. Other basic services were provided for the almost 1,000 apartments in the four hotels.

Even as repurposed for long-term housing, the hotels had innovative designs. Their concave shapes provided light and air, and they had translucent panels on the staircases, sky-lit domes, gardens, and play areas. Building elements included steel, glass, and reinforced concrete—for public housing, all innovative materials at the time. The hotels remain, even today, compelling physical testaments to the passion for urban planning that was a facet of Italian Fascism.

GETTING BACK

Cross Piazza E. Biffi. As you do, you'll see an underground parking garage (very fashionable these days, and often unpopular with area residents) and a bit of Roman ruins. Don't forget to look back, once across Piazza E. Biffi, for a great view of the red hotel. Walk left on Circonvallazione Ostiense, the biggest street you've seen on this itinerary, four short blocks to the cross street just before the bridge. There are many cafés and restaurants on this large boulevard. As you approach via G. Pullino, take a good look at this Santiago Calatrava-like bridge that opened in 2012, crossing the extensive railroad and Metro tracks and, after 90 years, joining Garbatella with the Ostiense neighborhood. Turn left on via Pullino. The Garbatella Metro stop is a short block ahead.

Walk 2

EUR

Mid-Century Spectacle

EUR. The letters refer to *Esposizione Universale di Roma* (Rome Universal Exposition). But the place, EUR, has two meanings, two sides, neither contained nor fully represented by those letters. Today it is the thriving center of business and government that it became in Italy's "boom" of the 1950s and 1960s: office towers, men in coats and ties lunching under the porticoes, shops for the well-dressed, condominiums and stand-alone houses, good schools, spaces for the kids to play, a lagoon with boat rentals, a prominent, architecturally significant stadium where all the big acts perform. The ideal upper-middle-class suburb. The suburb as spectacle.

The other meaning of EUR takes us deep inside the Fascist regime of dictator Benito Mussolini. Mussolini was at once a propagandist, a builder (which in Rome's center meant he also had many things torn down), and a man of brazen self-confidence. In mid-1935, in the 13th year of Fascism, and in the midst of a war in North Africa to make Abyssinia (Ethiopia) a colony, the Duce started planning for something akin to a world's fair on the city's southern edge. Like the fairs held in Chicago in 1933 and New York in 1939. Except this one would be permanent. The *esposizione* (exhibition, "E") would be held in Fascism's 20th year—dating from the March on Rome in 1922—that is, in 1942 ("42"). So what would become EUR was known then as "E42."

It is difficult to overestimate the brash exuberance, the burgeoning nationalism, the arrogance of authority and power that underlay these plans, and all that is there to behold in today's EUR. These qualities had been present in Fascism from its beginnings, of course, and one can see the results elsewhere in Rome, from the *Foro Mussolini* (1928, now *Foro Italico,* part of Walk 3 below; *Foro* means Forum) to the opening of the widened via del Mare (1930, now, in Rome's center, via del Teatro di Marcello) and via del'Impero (Empire Way, 1932, now via dei Fori Imperiali [Way of the Imperial Forums]; *Impero* means Empire); to the new town of Sabaudia (founded 1934), among others in the Agro Pontino, the malaria-ridden marshland south of Rome.

What was new by mid-decade was the sense that Italy's destiny was abroad, that the country was on the cusp of joining the ranks of the great world powers and playing in a league with the big boys. Italy's Fascist leaders looked toward partnership with Germany and, with the 1936 conquest of Ethiopia, toward expanding the country's North African empire, all in the service of recapturing the imperial glories of ancient Rome.

This vision—it proved to be a fantasy, and a destructive one at that—has everything to do with the look and feel of the EUR you'll experience on this itinerary. Until 1935, the architecture of Fascism was the product of modernist architects, like Mario De Renzi and Adalberto Libera, for whom Fascism was a forward-looking, business-oriented movement best represented by a rationalist architecture that emphasized functionality and simplicity. The post office on via Marmorata (near the Pyramid, designed by De Renzi and Libera), one of four architecturally significant Fascist-era post offices built in Rome in the 1930s, is a good example. By 1936, the rationalists had been pushed aside—although not entirely—by another group of architects, led by Marcello Piacentini, who, like Mussolini, saw Fascism as building on the strengths of Imperial Rome, and therefore best represented by an architecture that evoked those Roman roots and emphasized, above all else, monumentality. Piacentini was EUR's chief architect. Let's see what he produced.

GETTING THERE

EUR is accessible at three Metro stops on the B (blue) line. Get off at the third one, Fermi. See Walk 2 Map.

WHEN TO GO

Despite the porticoes, much of the itinerary is exposed; so in hot weather, morning is best. There are massive museums in EUR, and you may want to

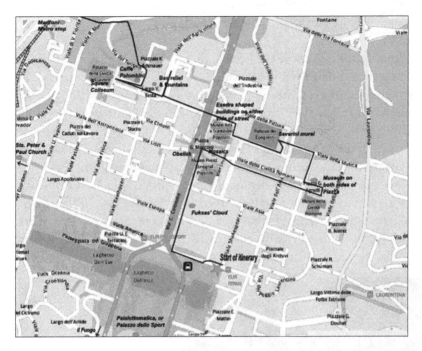

Walk 2 Itinerary

visit at least one of them; so plan accordingly. Don't go on a Monday, and check the museum times. Web sites are included below.

TO THE SEA

Once you've emerged from the Metro—you should be on the north side of viale America—walk across this small but busy two-lane street. (If you exit on the other side of viale America, you don't have to cross the street.) Find a place to look south, toward the lagoon below. It's artificial, created just for E42. Although today it's a space of play and leisure, when EUR was conceived it also had a symbolic function. As Italy re-imagined its future as a world power, its relationship to water, to the Mediterranean and oceans beyond, took on new importance. Ancient Rome had been a great sea power, and EUR was designed to recapture symbolically that role, orienting Rome once again toward the water, toward the ancient port of Ostia, toward a new naval presence. The lagoon—otherwise an attractive anomaly—spoke of those dreams.

SYMMETRICAL EUR

From your perch above the lagoon, or from a glance at any map, it will be apparent that EUR is a symmetrical place. It's divided, right down the center, by via Cristoforo Colombo (before 1948 it was, appropriately, via Imperiale: "Imperial Way"). When via Cristoforo Colombo splits as it crosses the lagoon, the two sides embrace the *Palazzo dello Sport,* perfectly centered. Designed by Pier Luigi Nervi for the 1960 Olympic games, the image of the building, distributed world-wide, became the symbol, writes historian Susan Schafer, "of a New Rome and with that a New Italy…fully purged of its Fascist past." *Palazzo dello Sport* has been renamed in an even more contemporary mode, marking EUR's business side, with advertising branding for the state lottery, *Palalottomatica.*

Palazzo dello Sport

The symmetry was important. As any dictator would, Mussolini detested disorder, even, perhaps especially, in the organization of urban space. He and other Fascists found Rome's dense, complex neighborhoods threatening, and the regime did its best to get rid of them, creating the broad boulevards that reveal (and in some cases buried) the city's ancient monuments. With EUR, the planners produced an urban plan that featured the social safety of openness and symmetry.

THE *FUNGO*

To the right (west) of the *Palazzo dello Sport* is another Rome icon, and another building you won't see up close on this itinerary: *Il Fungo* (the mushroom). The *Fungo* came about in the late 1950s, when the folks who were developing EUR faced two problems: First, they wanted more green space but needed a way to water it to keep it green; and second, they were concerned about the area's ability to fight fires. The *Fungo,* essentially a water tank, was the solution. Completed in 1960, the 160-foot (50-meter) tower has eight five-sided pilasters, supporting not only the tank but an upscale restaurant. The building was featured in several films, including Michael Antonioni's *L'Eclisse* (*The Eclipse*) [1962], in which the *Fungo* stands for the alienation produced by modern life—and perhaps also, in its shape, for the threat of nuclear annihilation. Visiting the *Fungo* turns

Il Fungo

out to be not all that depressing. There's a bar at the base and covered tables outside. If you go over to the *Fungo,* on the walk over or back spend a few moments deciphering the curious sculpture on the hillside next to the road. Designed by Ugo Attardi to celebrate the bicentennial of the storming of the Bastille, it's called "Vessel of the [French] Revolution."

FUKSAS' CLOUD

Let's move on. Head right (west) to via Cristoforo Colombo, and then again right (north), away from the lagoon. The sidewalk is surprisingly narrow, with some reprieve provided by a gas station. If you have children with you, hold tight to their hands for a block or two. While holding tight, don't

One of EUR's architecturally
significant stairways

miss the creative, modernist stairways that are a feature of EUR's architecture. There's a nice example on the *Poste Italiane* (Italian Postal Service) building—the first skyscraper on the left (west) across via Cristoforo Colombo.

The first cross street is viale Europa. To your left, up the hill (about a 10-minute walk, not on the itinerary) is the Church of Saints Peter and Paul (begun 1938, completed 1955); these are considered "Rome's saints." The church is a good example of Fascist efforts to incorporate Catholicism. Continue north. The block between viale Europa and the next cross street, viale Asia, is occupied by the construction site for Massimiliano Fuksas' Cloud, which is somewhere between dream and reality, art and architecture, fantasy and convention center. Even under construction it's weird and impressive, and you can get a good idea of what the final product is supposed to look like from the posters around the site. Of course, once it's completed you'll have to go in and look around.

Fuksas' Cloud, under construction

Born and educated in Rome, Fuksas is a loner type and a big idea guy. "All my life," he has said, "I have fought against form, shape and style," and he denies any evolution to his work. "I use a different language each time." He admits to a fondness for the artistry of Francesco Borromini, and perhaps we'll see echoes in the finished Cloud of the latter's famous 1626 *Palazzo Barberini* staircase in central Rome.

PIAZZA MARCONI, THE OBELISK, AND THE ARCH THAT ISN'T

Another block north past viale Asia brings us to Piazza Guglielmo Marconi, a grand and impressive plaza that centers EUR along both its north/south and east/west axes. Designed by a team of architects—Francesco Fariello, Saverio Muratori, and Ludovico Quaroni—it was begun in 1938, the year Hitler visited Rome, and completed in 1942, the year before Italy abandoned the war and the Germans occupied the city. It is named for the Nobel-prize winning engineer who is viewed as the father of radio. Marconi (1875–1937) joined the Fascist Party and was heralded by Mussolini. He is still revered in Italy; hence the piazza continues to bear his name. Today, the buildings on your side of the piazza are occupied by

Art and the obelisk

large state museums: to the north, the *Museo delle Arti e Tradizioni Popolari* (Museum of Popular Arts and Traditions—essentially folk culture; its Web site is sometimes available, but only in Italian); and, to the south, the *Museo Preistorico Etnografico Pigorini* (Luigi Pigorini National Museum of Prehistory and Ethnography; its Web site is not functional, but for information on this highly regarded museum, see the Asia-Europe Museum Network site).

The obelisk at the center was something of an afterthought; it was not installed until 1959. The original idea, in the 1930s, was that the piazza would be spanned from east to west by a giant triumphal arch, recalling the storied conquests of ancient Rome and that empire's triumphal arches, such as the Arch of Constantine alongside the Coliseum. In some sketches and posters, the proposed arch resembles the arch completed in St. Louis in 1966; in others the arch is a simple semi-circle. Whatever the configuration, and whatever material—cement, metal, or both—the span proved beyond the abilities of Italian engineers, and plans for it were dropped. In 1948, when Eero Saarinen won the competition for the St. Louis Gateway Arch with a design that closely resembled a poster by Ludovico Quaroni, some critics wondered whether his design was somehow Fascist, or Fascist-inspired. Although there is no definitive evidence linking the two, any arch built under Fascism would have had imperial connotations, and the 1948 competition—for an arch to commemorate the Louisiana Purchase—was about celebrating America's 19th-century western empire.

MOSAICS

Take a direct right (east) from the obelisk, walking toward and through the columns ahead. Once through the columns, don't miss the stunning wall mosaics on both sides of the passage. Both were completed in 1942. The one on the right, titled "Arts, Trades, Professions," is by the well-known Futurist, Fortunato Depero. Depero and Giacomo Balla were painters who signed the manifesto for the Futurist movement, which in the 1920s and 1930s was closely identified with Fascism, sharing its values of speed and movement. Look on the right half of this mosaic for three *fasci* in the design. Depero is also well known for his 1932 design of the Campari Soda bottle, still in production. The mosaic on

Depero mosaic

the left (north), titled "The Corporations," is by Enrico Prampolini, also a Futurist, though less well-known than Depero. Like many Futurist artists

31

and many Fascists, Prampolini was fascinated with flight and airplanes, an interest rather obliquely reflected in this work.

FASCIST MONUMENTALISM

Leaving the wall mosaics, continue east, slightly uphill along the divided viale della Civiltà Romana, to the next set of columns, which line the back wall of Piazza Giovanni Agnelli. The piazza is named for one of the founders of FIAT, a businessman, which tells you something about EUR today. These columns, and the museum buildings to the left and right (1939–52), constitute the best example in all of Rome of late Fascism's devotion to a monumental architecture that would signify and advertise Fascist state power. Imagine the piazza without automobiles and scooters. Awesome.

Fascist monumentalism

Although the columns at the end of the piazza don't resemble those of ancient Rome, this elevated area is sometimes used as a set for films about that era.

The *Museo della Civiltà Romana* (Museum of Roman Civilization) is located on both sides of the piazza. Through the entrance to the right

Film set at Piazza Agnelli

(note the iconography of Fascism: the eagles, the enormous doors) is the ticket office; through the entrance to the left is a massive scale model of ancient Rome—*da non perdere* (not to be missed). If you've spent any time in the Forum, this model is worth the price of admission. The Romans have carped for years that, because it is so interesting and evocative, the model should be more centrally located, but it continues to sit out here in EUR. The museum itself is somewhat disappointing—mostly copies—though the kids might enjoy the medieval weapons and touchable artifacts. For information, see the museum's Web site.

PALAZZO DEI CONGRESSI

When you've had your fill of the monumental, turn back toward the obelisk, continuing this time on the north (right) side of Piazza Agnelli. Take the first right (via dell'Architettura) and walk one long block amidst substantial postwar residences to the T at viale della Musica. Here, and elsewhere in the area, you'll

Vintage E42

find grates and manhole covers marked "E42"—quotidian objects, forged in the Fascist era. Turn left onto viale della Musica. Just a block straight ahead is one of EUR's most famous buildings: the *Palazzo dei Congressi*.

A GINO SEVERINI MURAL

You're approaching from the back, but in this case there's a reward. The rear hall/reception area—if the door isn't locked, walk in—contains a remarkable mural, running the width of the *Palazzo*. Gino Severini (1883–1966) completed it in 1953, the same year the building opened. Severini was deeply influenced by Futurism and Cubism, and he was close friends with Amedeo Modigliani. There is evidence of these influences in this work, ac-

Detail, Severini mural

complished for the Federation of Agricultural Enterprises and employing a motif based on the seasons.

Enjoy the mural, but don't miss getting a good look at the splendid building in which it is housed. Exit the back of the *Palazzo* toward the right and walk around the *Palazzo* to Piazza John F. Kennedy, where, ideally, the fountains are flowing and you'll find a couple of cafés for a late morning coffee.

ADALBERTO LIBERA'S *PALAZZO*

The architect of the *Palazzo dei Congressi* (Convention Building), one of the original EUR structures, was Adalberto Libera. In the late 1920s, Libera was one of the founders of the Italian Movement for Rational Architecture, based in Rome. He was influenced by both Futurism and Rationalism and maintained close ties with the Mussolini government. Here he managed to produce a building that spoke to Piacentini's fondness for monumentalism (the steps, the columns), while remaining true to his modernist preferences.

The *Palazzo* has many features, but none so obvious or original as that big cube in the middle, which houses the *Salone dei Ricevimenti* (Reception Hall). The cube is 400 square feet (36 square meters), pre-

Palazzo dei Congressi

cisely large enough to hold the Pantheon. The rounded top may have been necessary to bring the cube to Pantheon dimensions, but whatever its purpose, it is the signature feature. We have heard that the empty slab projecting from the front was to have supported a statue of Mussolini, but confirmation of this story has eluded us.

Take the street that runs west out of Piazza Kennedy, viale della Civiltà del Lavoro, with the *Palazzo dei Congressi* at your back. You're headed for that curious building in the distance, the one with all the arches. As you cross via Cristoforo Colombo, note the matching hemispheric buildings to your right, on the east and west sides of the multilane avenue. The hemisphere (*esedra*) is an iconic Roman architectural form; recall center Rome's Piazza della Repubblica, once called Piazza

Manikins power lunching on via Cristoforo Colombo

dell'Esedra, and laid out on the *esedra* shape of one of the halls of the Diocletian Baths.

The street you're on—still viale della Civiltà del Lavoro—is full of restaurants and cafés. We recommend you pass them by for a more interesting spot soon to come on this itinerary, with one exception. The *Futurarte Café* has prints and posters of the Futurists, many of which are accessible to the browser without dining there. Just beyond the café is one of EUR's few *nasoni* ("big noses," outdoor drinking fountains).

A SCULPTED HISTORY OF ITALY

You're now at the east end of a large rectangular piazza. Cross it to the north side and turn right onto via Ciro il Grande, which fronts an L-shaped

Detail, Morbiducci's *bas reflief* history of Rome

building with elaborate fountains and mosaics (1937–39). To the left of the fountains, a covered entrance contains a massive tablet of travertine marble, on which Publio Morbiducci has sculpted the history of Rome, beginning at the top with Romulus and Remus, continuing through Giuseppe Garibaldi's 19th-century efforts to unify Italy, and concluding with the Fascist era, Mussolini on horseback in Fascist salute.

THE SQUARE COLISEUM

Return to the piazza (head back on via Ciro il Grande and take a right at the boulevard viale della Civiltà del Lavoro) and the building at its end: the *Palazzo della Civiltà del Lavoro* (1938–43), also known as *Palazzo della Civiltà Italiana* (Building of Italian Civilization), or simply the Square Coliseum. It was designed by G. Guerrini, E. B. Lapadula, and M. Romano—none of them particularly well-known

The Square Coliseum

beyond this exceptional structure. For many years the building was all but obscured by reconstruction efforts, and in 2013, when we last saw it, a fence remained, making it difficult to see the 28 statues that occupy arches on the first floor, representing trades, fields of study, or larger social concepts such as politics and heroism. More accessible are the equestrian sculptures at the four corners of the base, by Morbiducci and Alberto Felci, of mythical Greek heroes, sons of Zeus and Leda. The inscription at the top reads: "A People of Poets, Artists, Saints, Thinkers, Scientists, Sailors, Explorers."

The Square Coliseum has been featured in many films, including *Rome, Open City* (1945) and *Boccaccio '70* (1962). It may or may not be true that the total number of the façade's six stories and nine arches refers to the number of letters in Benito and Mussolini. But there is no doubt of the building's ideological function or motivating concept: to recall the Coliseum, and by doing so, capture Fascist Rome's link to the ancients.

Some observers have trouble getting beyond the structure's Fascist origins, referring to it as "weird," "disturbing," "ugly," "creepy," and even "Soviet" in style. We prefer to emphasize the stunning harmony of its proportions. Fascism's architects were among the best in the world at the time, and nowhere is that more obvious than here, at the Square Coliseum.

CAFFÈ PALOMBINI

Ready for a bite to eat? Remarkably, you can have lunch or just a coffee at what was once the "official" restaurant of E42. Today it has a new name—*Caffè Palombini,* for the coffee people who own it—but it retains

Caffè Palombini

much of the aura of the early 1940s, when it was constructed. You're right on top of the café; just put your back to the Square Coliseum, walk to the first street on your left (Piazzale Adenauer) and turn in. The food is good, not particularly expensive, and you can order cafeteria-style or from a waiter at one of the inside or outside tables.

Fegarotti's inlaid marble mosaic, inside *Caffè Palombini*

Whether you dine here or not, don't miss what remains of the café's original art work. Straight ahead as you enter are some lovely frescoes by Franco Gentilini. The real prize is in a small room to the right of the entrance, sometimes occupied by diners, but public space nonetheless. At the end of that room is a gorgeous mosaic by Eugenio Fegarotti. Fegarotti was the recipient of significant Fascist patronage but, not being a member of the Party, he eventually lost his teaching position at Rome's Fine Arts Academy. This mosaic is on the theme of the restaurant and EUR; it features a table with cutlery and flowers and EUR's buildings in the background, all in polychromatic marble.

HOW TO GET BACK

Another surprise: at *Caffè Palombini* you're only a short walk from Metro stop EUR Magliana, the same line (Metro B) you came in on, but a different stop, closer to the center of Rome. To get there, turn left as you exit the restaurant, then left again at the corner (via del Turismo). Follow the stairs and path that go west, downhill. Enjoy the sculptures, including the highly stylized *bas relief* slab, as you descend. You'll cross a busy street (use the crosswalk) and enter a second part of the park. Follow the path as it curves left and then head for the large "wall" sculpture (another, larger *bas relief* slab) on the rise ahead. By Italian Ercole Drei, it was sculpted in 1940–42 on the theme of agriculture and crafts, but not installed until 1962 in this park, *Parco del*

Ercole Drei's "wall" sculpture

Turismo (Tourism Park). Go to the left in back of the wall sculpture and bear left on the path. You'll see a set of stairs leading to the busy street in front of the Magliana Metro stop. At your left there's a light and an underpass to cross that street.

FROM MUSSOLINI TO *MAXXI*

The Changing World of Flaminio

Until recently, Flaminio—a neighborhood, shaped like a light bulb, running north from Piazza del Popolo—remained a tourist backwater: a few bustling streets, a military installation, the curious housing complex (and a significant small arena) built for the 1960 Olympics. And just across the *Tevere,* the *Foro Italico,* a sprawling sports facility, also used for the games, but mostly constructed in the 1930s by Mussolini's government—a reminder of those dark days when Italians were drawn to dictatorship, colonialism, and war.

All of that is still there, including the *Foro Italico* (originally the *Foro Mussolini*; *foro* means forum), its Fascist origins made even more obvious by the controversial refurbishing of a giant obelisk to the Duce. Fascism in your face.

But there is also a new Flaminio. In less than a decade, two cultural centers, one for art and one for music, each designed by a world-famous architect, have changed the look and tone of the area, transforming it into a space of high culture and contemporary modernism. Flaminio is now chic—well, almost.

This new walk is a sort of double itinerary. You could approach it in two separate tours: one of Flaminio proper, the neighborhood that now features two of the most prominent cultural spaces of modern Rome; and the other, *Foro Italico*—the Fascist-era sports complex, now home to international sports competitions as well as Rome's two soccer teams. These arts and sports complexes are visually stunning architecture. And the performances and displays within them are often world-class. The venues signal the emergence of Rome as a modern city.

HOW TO GET THERE

Take tram #2 from Piazzale Flaminio, just outside the *porta* of Piazza del Popolo (sad to say, in front of the Burger King). This is a frequent tram, a recently refurbished line, and it's easy to hop on and off. We recommend you get off at Piazza Apollodoro (the fourth stop), on viale Tiziano (which the tram travels "out"). The tram returns to the Centro on the parallel via Flaminia. See below for alternative tram stops to see the Etruscan museum, or to get a good *cornetto*. See Walk 3 Itinerary.

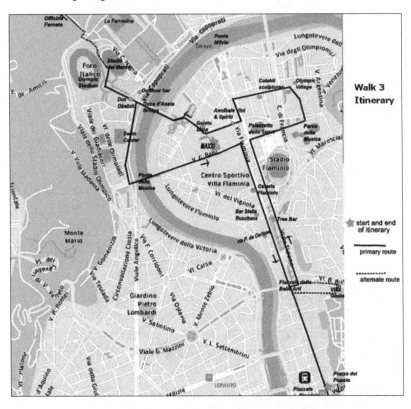

WHEN TO GO AND WHAT TO BRING

This itinerary features a lot of walking, so wear your walking shoes. It has many food and drink places along the way; you don't need to bring your own. Do go when the art museum *MAXXI* is open (not Mondays), even if you don't intend to pay the entrance fee. Depending on your taste for crowds, you might want to avoid—or plan to be among—the rowdy Sunday afternoon soccer fans during the season.

AN IMMEDIATE ALTERNATIVE STOP

The tram that takes you from Piazzale Flaminio to the heart of the Flaminio quarter trundles by the street leading to the marvelous Etruscan museum of *Villa Giulia*. To go to the museum, take the tram one stop, then walk in the direction of the tram to the intersection with via di Villa Giulia. This corner features a monumental fountain for Pope Julius III (*Giulio*), for whom the street and villa are named. Turn right (east) and walk up to the Pope's imposing "pleasure" villa (there weren't even rooms for staying overnight), built in the early 1550s. The Etruscan collection has been remounted and re-curated and is spectacular, even to those of us who don't often dip into ancient history. This national museum warrants more than RST's usual 40-minute museum stop. If you are adding this to the walk, you'll need all day. The museum is closed Mondays. Web site in Italian only, it appears. We suggest you use an Internet translation program to get the information in English.

Nymphaeum, *Villa Giulia*

To pick up the itinerary, get back on the tram by walking down viale delle Belle Arti and taking a right at the broad Piazzale delle Belle Arti. The tram stop is just ahead along the green space. Take it two stops to Piazza Apollodoro, in front of the round indoor arena. If you are still looking for your morning *cornetto,* get off the tram one stop earlier, at Piazza Ankara. Across the street on the northwest corner of via Flaminia and via Cesare Fracassini is *Bar Stella Ruschena.* They bake their own *cornetti,* and you can sit down without an extra charge.

THE REAL START

Take the tram from Piazzale Flaminio four stops to Piazza Apollodoro, in front of the round sports arena. As you stand at the piazza, you can orient yourself in four directions to worthy sites. In front of you, to the right (east) is the *Palazzetto dello Sport,* by the noted Italian engineer/architect of the 1960 Olympics, Pier Luigi Nervi. In back of you, on the same side of viale Tiziano, is the open air *Stadio Flaminio,* also by Nervi. More interesting than the current stadium is its predecessor, which featured a grand entrance dominated by four large columns topped with marvelous sculptures by Amleto Cataldi (we will find some of those later on this itinerary). That entrance appeared in neorealist filmmaker Vittorio De Sica's 1948 *The Bicycle Thief.* So, yes, you are at the heart of one of the great Italian films of all time, and of the 1960 Olympic Games. Directly to your right, farther along, is Renzo Piano's 2002 music complex, *Parco della Musica,* and directly to your left, again farther along, is *MAXXI,* Zaha Hadid's 2010 contemporary arts building. Those two complexes—by two of Rome's "Starchitects"—are both on this itinerary, so more will be said later. Piazza Apollodoro has a kiosk bar/café where you can stop for refreshments.

PALAZZETTO DELLO SPORT

Our first stop is the *Palazzetto dello Sport* (1956/57). The designer, Pier Luigi Nervi, was an engineer, one especially skilled in the use of prefabricated, reinforced concrete. Here, he was able to use the weighty material to produce volume and, more remarkably, a sense of openness and movement. He used similarly creative methods in designing other buildings for the 1960 Olympic Games in Rome, including the *Palazzo dello Sport* in EUR, south of the city center. The curving, weight-bearing struts of the *Palazzetto's* innovative dome bring to mind the flying buttresses with which Nervi's Renaissance predecessors held up the walls of their cathedrals.

Pier Luigi Nervi's *Palazzetto dello Sport*

Although the *Palazzetto* may seem to need TLC and restoration—the roof was peeling and shabby when we last saw it—it's a worthy building, especially given its construction at a time when modernism's search for its future produced much that was awkward. It's usually open and you can poke around inside to get a feel for its golden windows and large, uninterrupted interior space. The lower half of the dome has a continuous ribbon of window around the entire building, producing some lovely visual effects—inside during the day, outside at night. Avery Brundage, the hard-nosed head of the International Olympic Committee and not easily given to hyperbole, compared Nervi's structures to the works of "Bernini and Michelangelo, and the monuments left by Hadrian, Trajan, and other Caesars."

During the Olympics, the *Palazzetto* was used for boxing and basketball, among other events, so it's likely that Cassius Clay (soon to be Muhammad Ali) fought here and that Jerry West, Jerry Lucas, and Oscar

Robertson worked their magic on the *Palazzetto*'s basketball court. Organizers of the games, anxious to showcase Rome's ancient heritage, arranged to hold competitions at the Baths of Caracalla (gymnastics) and the Basilica of Maxentius in the Roman Forum (wrestling). One of the most dramatic and symbolic of the Olympic events, the marathon, run at night, began at Michelangelo's stairs at the *Campidoglio* (Capitoline Hill) and finished under torchlight at the Arch of Constantine—an "arch of triumph" used as a symbol by the Fascists as well as the ancients. In an ironic and poignant twist, the winner of the race was Ethiopian Abebe Bikila, whose country had been brutally conquered and occupied by the Fascists in 1936. Bikila ran barefoot.

CORSO DI FRANCIA

You've taken a right turn off the piazza to examine the *Palazzetto*. Continue along this main drag, viale P. de Coubertin. Don't neglect to look up as you cross under the immense viaduct of the highway corso di Francia (1957/58), built for the Olympics to carry traffic from the Olympic sites on this side of the *Tevere* to the *Foro Italico* and venues on the other side. The viaduct was elevated, and placed on single pilasters, precisely to avoid its becoming a great barrier within the Olympic Village. All the prominent Italian architects and engineers of the period, including many who were active under Fascism, were involved in the Olympic sites, including this one. Nervi was engaged in the design and engineering of the viaduct, though architectural credit is usually given to Riccardo Morandi, who also designed a visually significant market (the circular parking garage is special) on via Magna Grecia in the Appio quarter of Rome. Note, too, that the pilasters of the *corso* have been remarkably well integrated into the entrance to *Parco della Musica,* just ahead.

The architects of the viaduct surely could not have anticipated one of its uses. At the games, the highway served as a natural divider between the women athletes, housed on its west side, and the men, housed to the east. In an era outstanding for its prudery, officials were concerned that the boys would get into the girls' rooms; so everything was gated, fenced, and guarded. Despite the precautions, Italian men found binoculars and telephoto lenses, parked their cars on the *corso,* and enjoyed the view.

PARCO DELLA MUSICA

As you finish crossing under corso di Francia, you are entering Renzo Piano's music complex, *Parco della Musica* (completed 2002), referred to by most Romans simply as the "Auditorium." We think it's one of Piano's best buildings; he designed the *New York Times* headquarters in New York City and the main addition to the Los Angeles County Museum of Art. We brought Parco della Musica in at #37 on Rome the Second Time's Top 40. As you walk along here, you'll see a restaurant/bar, *ReD,* that is popular and, for an hour or two in the late afternoon, features a reasonable *aperitivo*—drinks and snack buffet combo at a discount. There is also a small art gallery that has good exhibits from time to time, at little or no cost. The bookstore is comfortable and well stocked (a good place to find Italian music), but woefully short on books in anything but Italian.

Renzo Piano's *Parco della Musica*

As you round the corner after the bookstore, you enter the central "piazza" of Piano's creation, with views of the organic, mushroom- or turtle shell-like metal roofs of the three large performance halls, perhaps Piano's most important contribution to the architectural plasticity that

Frank Gehry has made famous in his Los Angeles Disney Concert Hall. There is a casual café/bar and ticket office to your right. You can go in and poke around this complex, which features the clever word plays of conceptual artist Jenny Holzer. There are tours, too, but generally only in Italian. The Web site lists coming events; click on the "Eng" button at top right. There are often free art exhibits within the complex, as well as a sixth-century BCE village that was unearthed in the construction of the *Parco.* For more on the pre-Roman village, see our post on then-Mayor Francesco Rutelli's story of its discovery.

OLYMPIC VILLAGE

Once you've explored *Parco della Musica,* head across the street and over the open green space in front of *Parco della Musica,* to the Olympic Village. We suggest wandering around a bit, getting a feel for this 1960 athlete housing, now somewhat tattered apartments. The Village was designed by a team of distinguished Italian architects, including Adalberto Libera, whose via Marmorata post office is one of the finest works of the Fascist era and who was one of the principal architects of EUR.

The Village buildings, especially in their current scruffy state, are not at the level of the post office; yet they have some interesting qualities. They vary in number of stories and in surface treatments. But all are in a modernist vocabulary common to the 1950s and early 1960s. Some of the buildings display their original pastel colors. Some are topped by impressive round constructions—ventilation systems, likely—that emphasize the rationalist, geometric character of the structures. Most if not all of the buildings are raised one story above ground, probably to give the Village a greater sense of integration and community and to prevent the buildings from becoming barriers to communication among the different nationalities encamped there for the games. The great American decathlon athlete, Rafer Johnson, was among those who found another benefit; on a Sunday before his event, he was seen relaxing in a lounge chair in the cool air under one of the structures, listening to jazz on a portable radio while clearing his mind for the rigors of competition. Besides the dormitories, the Village had shops, restaurants and sidewalk cafés, a bank, recreation rooms and cafeterias, an outdoor movie theater, and a dance floor, crowded every evening.

Among the self-made celebrities at the Olympic Village was a young

Cassius Clay. But Clay was not yet famous and not yet Muhammad Ali. The gold medal he would win in Rome would be his springboard to suc-

Amleto Cataldi sculpture, Olympic Village in back

cess and celebrity. Even so, Clay made a reputation in the Village and elsewhere, "always preaching," "always talking," as an American diver put it. In his entertaining book on the Rome Olympics, Rome 1960, David Maraniss tells the story of a naïve and thirsty Clay, drinking from the water fountain in his suite, unaware it was a bidet.

All the Village streets are named for countries or the Olympiad. Get yourself to the southeast corner of viale XVII Olimpiade and via Germania (about one to two blocks east of corso di Francia) and you'll see a hidden—often in the weeds—treasure of this area: one of Amleto Cataldi's sculptures from the 1927 stadium. There's another on via Unione Sovietica, about two blocks west of corso di Francia. We haven't found the remaining two. Cataldi is also the sculptor of the "tax man" statue on viale XXI Aprile, a short walk from Piazza Bologna.

WINE BAR SIGHTING

Keep heading west on viale XVII Olimpiade until you reach viale Tiziano (the street on which you stepped off the tram, but further north). Across via Flaminia and just a few steps back towards the center is Piazza dei Carracci. There's a good wine bar/café here—*Annibale Vini & Spiriti*. You may also note you have crossed over from streets named for countries and the Olympics, to streets named for Italian artists. The Carracci brothers—painters from Bologna—are the source of the piazza name, and *Annibale* (in English, Hannibal) was the first name of one of them. There's also an interesting shop of wine stoppers on the corner next to the wine bar.

Back entrance to *MAXXI*, not always open

Continue along the street to the left of the piazza, via Masaccio, as it doglegs right and then goes towards the large bridge, *Ponte Duca d'Aosta*. You will walk past the back entrance of *MAXXI*. The museum is later in this itinerary, but you can go in it from this entrance, which is not always open, if you want to explore it and its exhibitions at this point.

The street, which changes its name to via Luigi Poletti as it doglegs, sports a "natural" gelato shop; Neve di Latte, favored by Rome food writer Katie Parla, is located at no. 6.

PONTE DUCA D'AOSTA

If you haven't deviated from the itinerary by going to *MAXXI*, or if you are picking up where we last left you, continue on via Poletti and then straight across the park area to the edge of the *Tevere* and the imposing *Ponte Duca d'Aosta*. The bridge (*ponte*) was built by the Fascists in 1939–42, honoring Emanuele Filiberto, Second Duke of Aosta, a World War I general who was loyal to Mussolini. The statues and decorations on the bridge all commemorate Italy in World War I, a conflict it fought incompetently and with horrific losses, and exited with some humiliation, preparing the ground for Mussolini.

One of the *bas reliefs* says:

Tutti Eroi!
O il Piave
O tutti Accoppati!

Homage to Italian soldiers in World War I, *Ponte Duca d'Aosta*

Loosely translated: "All Heroes! The Piave or Death!" The Piave is the northeastern river that was the line the Italians finally held in their ignominious, helter-skelter retreat from the Austro-Hungarian armies. For a brief overview of the war in this zone, see RST's post.

Look upriver at the next bridge—the Ponte Milvio, a significant site in ancient Christian history. The first mention of a bridge at this spot is in 200 BCE, during the Second Punic War. In 300 CE, the Roman Emperor Constantine was successful here in his battle against Maxentius, and saw a vision of a cross, the first step in his conversion to Christianity. Today the bridge is festooned with padlocks signifying undying love, and the piazza on the north side is the site of Rome's biggest late-night party (known as a *movida*), to the disgruntlement of those who live nearby. One note of caution: at least one reader on TripAdvisor thought this area—including to the end of the tram line and the *Tevere* beyond it—threatening and full of homeless people. This is not our experience, and we haven't heard it from anyone else.

FORO ITALICO

Back to our bridge: going over the *Ponte Duca d'Aosta* gives you some idea of the concept behind Mussolini's *Foro Italico,* then called *Foro Mussolini* (Mussolini's Forum). This complex landed at #5 on Rome the Second Time's Top 40 list; that's how intrigued we are by it, though most guidebooks take no notice.

At the piazza on the other side of the bridge you will see— prominently—a tall obelisk (120 feet [35 meters], 770 tons [700,000 kilograms]) that has "MUSSOLINI—DUX" on it. The marble was quarried in the Apuane Alps, and according to historian T. Corey Brennan (in his 2010 essay, "The 1960 Rome Olympics: Spaces and Spectacle"), it proved enormously difficult to move the main 300-ton (275,000-kilogram) shaft the first 1,000 feet (300 meters) in 10,000 man/days, and not much easier to mount it in the piazza. The date of the placement of the obelisk (1932, using the Fascist numbering system), and the name of the sponsoring organization (the *Opera Nazionale Balilla,* a group dedicated to the physical fitness of Italian youth), once appeared on the side of the piece but were removed just weeks before the 1960 games in a frenzy of worry that these signs of Fascism would reflect badly on the new Italian Republic. Even so, during the games the monu-

Controversial obelisk exalting Mussolini, in piazza named after anti-Fascist

ment remained an embarrassing reminder of Italy's infatuation with the Duce (dux is Latin, *duce* Italian—meaning leader), and some were inclined to tear it down. The obelisk survived, and with some controversy, was recently restored.

The piazza in which the obelisk stands is now called Piazza Lauro de Bosis. De Bosis, an Italian poet and aviator, won a silver medal in an Olympic arts competition (those were the days!) and died when his plane ran out of fuel as he was dropping anti-Fascist leaflets over Rome. So the naming of the piazza is clearly post-World War II. It was originally Piazza dell'Obelisco (referring to the obelisk) or, for architectural historians, Piazzale del Monolite (monolith). One of our favorite very casual places to stop and have a cool or hot drink, depending on the weather, is the riverside bar opposite the obelisk: *Pizza di buongustaio,* meaning "Gourmand's (better here, "Foodie's) pizza." It's small, but it has the essentials, including a clean bathroom. You can sit here and debate whether or not the obelisk should have been restored with Il Duce's name on it.

As you look at these buildings, which comprise a kind of Mussolini sports theme park, you can see the five intertwined Olympic rings—the Olympic symbol. On your left, a building is marked *CONI Piscine*; this is

Bar with a view—and a bathroom

the indoor swimming complex. We recommend you enter—just walk in—and see the beautiful 1937 mosaics around the pool. *CONI* refers to the Italian Olympic Committee: *Comitato Olimpico Nazionale Italiano*; *piscine* means swimming pools.

As Brennan explains, in the 1930s these buildings housed the *Accademia Fascista di Educazione Fisica* (Fascist Academy of Physical Education), a training center for the hundreds of physical education instructors who would staff the 890 *Balilla* houses (centers for the physical education of youth), 1470 gymnasiums, 2568 playing fields, and other facilities the Fascist regime claimed to have built. Mahatma Gandhi was sufficiently impressed to spend one of his two days in Rome in 1931 at the *Accademia,* talking with officials and chatting with the *Balilla* boys.

Then head straight behind the obelisk, taking care to avoid future Olympians practicing on their skateboards. Along this viale del Foro Italico—a walking street now, and once called viale del *Foro Mussolini*—are large marble blocks designed (by Luigi Moretti) to commemorate Fascism's triumphs, including the acquisition of its North African colonies. If they are free of graffiti, which is not always, you can read

Mosaics at 1937 pool mix athletes and mythology

older ones, like *"XV NOV MCMXIIII MUSSOLINI FONDA IL POPOLO D'ITALIA"*—Nov. 15, 1914, Mussolini founds the newspaper, Il Popolo d'Italia; or *"XXVIII OTT MCMXXII MARCIA SU ROMA"*—Oct. 28, 1922, The March on Rome; and *"IX MAGGIO XIV E.F. L'ITALIA HA FINALMENTE IL SUO IMPERO"*—May 9, Fascist Era 14 (i.e., 1936), Italy finally has its Empire. The date 1936 refers to the acquisition of Ethiopia, conquered with the use of poison gas. You will notice many blank marbles as well; fortunately, Mussolini was stopped before he could do more damage. The *Foro* was inaugurated in 1932 on November 4, a date marking Italy's "victory" in the renamed town of Vittorio

Fascist iconography underfoot in *Foro Italico: fascio*, eagle, and "M" for Mussolini

Veneto, in World War I. As on the *Ponte Duca d'Aosta,* one can see Mussolini's effort to reclaim glory from the tragic trajectory of that war.

OLYMPIC STADIUM AND *STADIO DEI MARMI*

You now should be at the circle in front of Olympic Stadium. Constructed in the 1930s, the stadium was remodeled for the 1960 games, then again in the 1990s, when the tent-like roof was added. It was here, in 1960, that the elegant and popular sprinter Wilma Rudolph won gold at 100 and 200 meters. But it may be of more significance that during the opening ceremonies for the games, decathlete Rafer Johnson entered *Stadio Olimpico* as the first black athlete to represent his team—and the United States—by carrying the American flag.

The stadium now sits above ground, blocking the view of Monte Mario behind it, unlike its original siting. Hitler was entertained here in spectacular fashion during his May 1938 visit to Rome. Following the "standard" show featuring thousands of people marching around and a surfeit of eagles and swastikas, the Führer and the Duce turned their attention to the side of Monte Mario—then visible, obviously—for a grand staged performance of a German opera, Richard Wagner's *Lohengrin.* What fun.

As we noted, the stadium is home to both of Rome's soccer teams, Roma and Lazio, although Roma is contemplating finding its "own" stadium elsewhere (Say it isn't so, Roma!). You can't get in the stadium, even to look around, without a ticket to a game or concert.

To the right of Olympic Stadium is the 1932 *Stadio dei Marmi*—the Stadium of Marbles, or marble statues. This you usually can get into, and it's a photographer's dream, although the sculpting—all done on location in the marble region of northern Tuscany—is not considered of the highest quality. The overall architect was Enrico Del Debbio, who was the chief designer of most of *Foro Mussolini.* The Italian provinces sponsored individual statues, rendered in Greek form, that represent different sports. There's a lot of Carrara marble here! Considered by many the centerpiece of the *Foro,* the statues to one art historian "appear to be the direct descendants of the heroes of Italy's countless war memorials.... The poses of the wrestlers, archers, and slingers, with arms raised and ready to throw whatever it is they throw, are closely related to those of the soldiers also naked (except for their helmets), who thrust their chest toward the enemy as they hurl their last grenade." Others who have studied these sculptures see in

Stadio dei Marmi

them the feral young men in Pasolini movies; still others think that the naked men (fig leaves were added and quickly removed after World War II) represent Italy's hope in success as a colonizer. During the 1960 games the stadium was an active venue, hosting field hockey competitions and track and field athletes warming up while awaiting their events at the big stadium beyond. Today the *Stadio dei Marmi* is used for the occasional athletic event, but it is primarily of aesthetic value.

Everywhere you look or walk in this *Foro,* you will find statues, sculptures, buildings of interest. Off in the distance to the north is still another Del Debbio building, conceived in 1937 as the headquarters of the Fascist Party (and as the biggest building in Italy), but not finished until 1956. It now houses the Italian Ministry of Foreign Affairs, called the Farnesina.

OFFICINE FARNETO

We recommend a side-trip in back of the *Foro,* beyond the big stadium, to some of the outbuildings. These too are by Del Debbio, and one, a former warehouse, has been recently restored with private funds. The five-minute walk to these buildings is up via dei Monti della Farnesina. At the bend in the road, no. 77, you can't miss *Officine Farneto,* a stunning example of Del Debbio's talents, a masterpiece of rationalist, curvilinear modernism. The complex has become a chic spot for small conferences

Officine Farneto

and well-attended fashion shows. The owners might give you a tour (they did us). There is also a small café here, sometimes open.

A BRIDGE TOO FAR?

You've made it to the end of *Foro Italico*. Trace your steps back to the *Tevere* and the *Ponte Duca d'Aosta*—but don't cross it. Stay on the west bank of the river and walk about 10 minutes downriver to the next bridge. This is yet another Santiago Calatrava-inspired 2011 pedestrian bridge: *Ponte della Musica* (Music Bridge). It is the first public pedestrian bridge to cross the *Tevere* since the Roman Empire. Dianne rather likes it. Bill does too, though he thinks it may deserve its nickname as "the bridge to nowhere." The nowhere is where you are.

STARCHITECTURE: *MAXXI*

Cross the bridge and take a direct line across the piazza to via Guido Reni. Within a few blocks you'll arrive at the main entrance, on your left, to *MAXXI,* the national contemporary art gallery. The XXI in the name sig-

The allure of *MAXXI* at night

nifies the 21st century. While its exhibitions are uneven and its collection paltry for a national gallery, the building by Zaha Hadid, the Pritzker Prize-winning architect who won the competition among 273 candidates, is spectacular. Whether one likes this massive structure, which opened in 2010, or not, thinks it's functional or not, believes it integrates with the neighborhood or not, is a different story. We have had these debates on the RST blog. Be sure to enter the museum and look around on the ground floor, which you can do without buying a ticket for the current exhibitions. The exterior space at the rear of the building is redesigned from time to time and is usually worth exploring. For hours, exhibitions, and programs, check *MAXXI*'s Web site.

THE WAY HOME, PLACES TO EAT

To get home, wherever that may be, return to the via Guido Reni entrance to *MAXXI* and continue in the direction you had been walking (away from the *Tevere*) to via Flaminia, where you can pick up the tram. Or, if you want to stop at the wine bar, or for a gelato, try the back entrance of the museum on via Masaccio. Sometimes open, sometimes not.

If it's lunch or dinner time, you can walk toward the center on via Flaminia or take the tram the same direction one stop toward Piazza del Popolo to go to one of several restaurants in the block bounded by via Flaminia, via Fracassini, via Tiepolo, and viale del Vignola. We add to those restaurants a suggestion from Katie Parla (www.parlafood.com) of a new restaurant on via Flaminia, between via Guido Reni and viale del Vignola: Osteria Flaminio, at no. 297.

THE BICYCLE THIEF

We can't let you go yet. If you still have some energy, continue on via Flaminia, just past *Tree Bar* (past via Fracassini) to via Pietro da Cortona. Take a right on this street and look at the first large doorway on your left (no. 1, almost to the next corner). That's the doorway where the second bicycle was stolen in Vittorio de Sica's 1948 neorealist gem, The Bicycle Thief (in Italian *The Bicycle Thieves*—an important difference).

Pick up the tram on via Flaminia back to Piazzale Flaminio. There's a stop at the piazza just before *Tree Bar,* or take a bus from the stop in front of the school just before via Pietro da Cortona.

Walk 4

THE STAIRS OF TRASTEVERE

JUST BEYOND THE once working-class Trastevere (literally, across the *Tevere,* or Tiber) area familiar to most tourists—bustling restaurants, wine bars, picturesque alleyways and squares, beer-drinking American youth—is another area across the Tiber, another Trastevere, known as the Gianicolo. It towers above the urban scene below, offering striking views of the city and environs. Although one can drive to the top from six or seven directions, the Gianicolo is also densely endowed with stairs, providing bold pedestrians with a way to surmount the numerous ridges that flow down from the top. On this itinerary, we're headed up—and down, and up—those stairs. Our main purpose is to offer an exhilarating physical experience. But if you're not too compulsive, not too eager to get to the next set of stairs, there are sights to be seen, some compelling, some spectacular.

We acknowledge this itinerary reflects a modern, West Coast (U.S.) culture: exercise and sightseeing at the same time. Books of "stairway walks" have been published for the cities of Seattle, San Francisco, and Los Angeles, for example. We hope to start a trend in Rome, and there is no better place to begin than what is sometimes called Rome's eighth hill.

Walking time: 1 hour (does *not* include time for stops, looking at views, etc.)

Ascending stairs: 717 (about 450 vertical feet, 140 meters)

Difficulty rating: moderately strenuous

Time to go: depart before 10 a.m. to insure access to a monument and a church late in the itinerary; avoid Mondays if you want to go inside the ossuary, which we recommend.

See Walk 4 Itinerary.

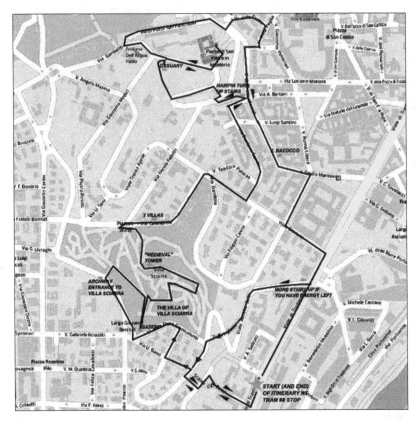

Walk 4 Itinerary

HOW TO GET THERE

Take the #8 tram from its end-of-the-line stop at Piazza Venezia or from
any of several stops at or near Largo di Torre Argentina or in the heart of
Trastevere. The walk begins at the corner of viale Trastevere and via Ugo
Bassi, opposite the tram stop Ippolito Nievo, to the right as you look up
the tram line.

UP WE GO

Ascend the staircase *Scalea Ugo Bassi*—4 sets of 21 steps each—then
right up a shallow and broad set of 13 steps. At the path, go left for
about 50 yards (meters) to a set of wooden steps with green iron rail-

Scalea Ugo Bassi

ings, and ascend (sets of 14, 9, 17, 16, 10, and 16 steps, 82 in all). Note the graffiti on the wall ahead (if it's still there): "Tassinaro Vive! C.M.L. '74," the words of radical (*ultra*) fans of the Lazio soccer club, celebrating their June 2013 victory over rival Roma and referring here to Lazio's first *Scudetto* (Italian championship) victory in 1974. Just to the right there are more steps (18, 18, 18, total 54), and once you climb them, a view of the gazometro (the round structure that once carried natural gas), the Ostiense bridge and, at left, the Alban Hills.

Hard-earned view

Just ahead, there's a *nasone* ("big nose"—a large nose-shaped fountain) where you can stop for a drink and catch your breath. This is still via Ugo Bassi.

Go right on via Aurelio Saffi. On the left, Villa Sara, with statuary. At the T, go left on viale delle Mura Gianicolensi and follow the city wall as it turns right. Note above, a plaque to Pope Urban VIII, a member of the Barberini family, and hence decorated with bees, the family symbol. And below, another plaque: SPQR 1839, referring to some city intervention on that date. To the left you'll see the Salvator Mundi hospital, with its rationalist, Fascist-era entrance and wall.

Entrance to Villa Sciarra

VILLA SCIARRA

Not far ahead on the right is a small entrance to the park of Villa Sciarra, first developed in the 1600s by the Barberini family. Go through the arch (note the Barberini bee above) and immediately take the path right. Not far ahead on the left, you'll pass a special semi-circular (*esedra*-shaped) garden holding 12 statues, each representing one month of the year, and several sculpted trees.

At this garden, take the shallow steps up right (28 of them), go left about 15 yards (meters), then follow the tiles right, past the dry fountain and up another 11 steps to the delightful gazebo with its iron cupola near the wall—nice views!

Retrace your steps (3 plus 8) and, at the end of the tiles, go right, following the path down left (8 cobblestone steps). At viale Adolfo Leducq (still in the park), turn right along the front of Villa Sciarra itself, now

Sculpture garden, Villa Sciarra

undergoing restoration. Since 1932 the impressive house has been the home of the Italian Institute for German Studies. A scene from the 1964 cult film *Sei Donne per L'Assassino* was shot here (literal translation, Six Women for the Assassin; the American title is *Blood and Black*

Gazebo cupola, Villa Sciarra

Lace). The park in which the structure is located was left by the widow of the American diplomat George Wurts—an avid gardener—to Benito Mussolini, on the condition that it become a public park. He, in turn, ceded it to the City of Rome. The park's dense wisteria (long gone, apparently, though we'll have to check in April), was the inspiration for one of Pier Paolo Pasolini's poems.

BERNINI AND PIACENTINI

Take the path around the nearby fountain, past the huge sawed-off tree trunk, to the right of the next fountain, and descend on the curving stairs (35 steps). At the path below, turn right and follow the wood railing on your left to the first opening, and descend (16 steps).

At the faux medieval tower (1910s) ahead, ascend the 14 steps and turn right, take the path about 15 yards (meters), then ascend again (8, 13, 8, 19 steps, total 48). At the top of this staircase, go left, past the pool high

Ascending stairway next to faux medieval tower

on the right, to the stairs, also on the right, and ascend (6, 4, 4, 6 steps, total 20). At the top, go straight a few paces to the main path and take it right, past another drinking fountain, and prepare to exit the park just ahead. Before you do so, admire the larger fountain here. Designed, according to one Monteverde historian, by Gianlorenzo Bernini, it features two small satyrs playing with a baby goat.

The entrance/exit portal is notable, too, if much more recent; it was designed in 1908 by Pio Piacentini, another notable Rome architect. The female figure was likely based on George's wife, Henrietta Tower Wurts. Both are buried in the Protestant cemetery in Testaccio, in the shadow of Rome's Pyramid.

THREE VILLAS

As you leave the park, take a hard right on via Calandrelli, downhill, past three sumptuous villas on the left: one with a modernist flair, another neo-classical (built in 1925), a third medieval in appearance. Note the sidewalk grates on this section of the street, complete with *fasci,* the Fascist symbol, indicative of the period in which these streets were laid out and the villas were built. If you're lucky and look ahead at just the right time, you can see the French academy, Villa Medici, far across Rome, perfectly framed by the trees.

A window on Villa Medici

At the T ahead, turn right briefly to the stairs on the left. From the top of the stairs, there's a nice view of the Palatine Forum at 10 o'clock. Descend (6 sets of 21 steps, total 126).

126 steps in descent

At the bottom, take an immediate left and walk straight for about one block, to the right of the rounded building on the left, then curve gently left and follow the street to the very end (it appears as if there is no exit, but there is). At the end of the street turn right on the cobblestones, then immediately left in a hairpin turn, and ascend the stairs at the corner (13, 6, 4, 27, then 6, 11 steps, total 67) to the road above. Go straight across the street (watch the traffic) and ascend more steps (8, 7, 7, 5, 5, 20 steps, total 52). At the top, turn left and follow the busy road to the curve. Ascend the stairs at the right (you'll have to cross the road to get to these—9, 10, 8, 11, 10, 24 steps, total 72).

A FASCIST-ERA OSSUARY

At the top, cross the grassy area at the right, next to the white monument. There's a small wet patch, caused by a spring or a pipe leak. Go to the

Roma o morte, one of Rome's least-known monuments

front of the monument and enter (open Tuesday-Sunday, 9 a.m.-1 p.m.). Be sure to go around back and below to the splendid gold-ceilinged ossuary. The structure honors those who died in the Risorgimento—the Italian unification movement of the mid-19th century—but it was built by Mussolini's Fascist regime in 1941.

A Roman friend fondly recalls playing soccer on the grassy spaces around the monument in the late 1960s, when he was a junior high student on via della Paglia, occasionally playing hookey. The call went out among the boys in dialect—*annamo* (in Italian, *andiamo*) *a oromaomorte,* the last word derived from the inscription on the monument: *o roma o morte* (Rome or Death). What it meant to the boys was simply "let's go play soccer on the fields around the monument."

Romulus, Remus, and the she-wolf, detail, ossuary

SAN PIETRO IN MONTORIO AND ACQUA PAOLA

Exiting the monument, turn right. Walk about 100 yards (meters) down the hill on via Garibaldi to the piazza coming in on the left. Enter the piazza, which is the front courtyard of the church, San Pietro in Montorio, and which looks out on a spectacular view of Rome. The church, rebuilt in

Groom checks cell phone at wedding shoot
at Bramante's *Tempietto*

the 15th century reputedly over the spot where Saint Peter was crucified, has a significant collection of Renaissance art, including works by Giorgio Vasari and Gianlorenzo Bernini. The real gem is the *Tempietto* (little temple) by Donato Bramante, in the courtyard to the right of the church's façade. Don't miss what is regarded as a perfect little building. Considered by some to be more sculpture than architecture, its interior is so small that it appears it was intended to be viewed from the outside. If you are counting your steps of ascent, add those going up to the *Tempietto* as well as the steps to the church and to the courtyard; they are not included in your 717.

After soaking in the art, architecture, and history here (there's a plaque to the Garibaldini, too), return the way you came, up via Garibaldi. About 100 yards (meters) past the ossuary is the Aqua Paola Fountain (*Fontana dell'Acqua Paola*), familiarly referred to as the *Fontanone*—"the really big fountain"—and, across the road, superb views of the city below. The Aqua Paola Fountain is a *mostre* or "show" fountain, designed to show off—as it comes into the city—

Acqua Paola

the aqueduct built by Pope Paul V (*Paolo,* hence *Acqua Paola*—Paul's Aqueduct). Look for the Borghese coat of arms, which includes a dragon and an eagle (Pope Paul V was from the Borghese family). You'll see dragons and eagles everywhere in this fountain. Despite the Pope's efforts, the water, which comes from Lake Bracciano, is not considered very good. So the phrase *acqua paola* means just that—something that's not very good, or even worthless.

From your position across the road from the fountain, follow the railing as it curves counterclockwise, then just up the road and sharply to the

It's all downhill

right, where there's a staircase. Descend (21, 23, 24, total 68 steps) and continue downhill on via di San Pancrazio to via Garibaldi. There's a 1937 (year XV of Fascism) drinking fountain on the right.

Turn right here for about 30 yards (meters) to the stairs on the left, and descend (25 plus 25 steps). At the bottom, take the right fork. Note the wall art on the right in the small piazza. At the T, turn right on via della Paglia. After a small piazza, bend right sharply, and ascend the stairs (8, 7, 15, 11 steps, total 41).

At the top of that staircase, go left, past the large fountain on the right, past the now familiar stairs on the right, down via Goffredo Mameli. On the left as you descend, you'll pass one of our favorite wine bars, Il Bacocco, at no. 61. Curve left, with the Carabinieri office on your left. Turn right on via Dandolo, where the back of the massive state education building will be on your left. Take a left at the next corner to viale Trastevere. There you turn right for one block to via Aurelio Saffi. If you've had enough stairs, you're close to a tram stop here. Simply walk up (away from the center) viale Trastevere about one block to the tram stop where you got off to start this walk.

CLIMBING AGAIN

Now begin the last part of this itinerary by a gradual ascent, using the sidewalk on the left. As the sidewalk ends, cross the street and ascend the stairs

Scala Righetto

of *Scala Righetto* (16, 16, 24 steps, total 56), cross the road and climb further (17, 29, 29 steps, total 75).

At the top, note the statue to the Virgin Mary in the small scruffy park, and across the street and just left, the 1960s building with its cool, modernist balconies. Follow the wall on the left side of the street to the now familiar wood stairs with metal railings, and descend these stairs (82 steps), then 13 shallow steps, then a total of 84 more in 4 sets of 21 steps to viale Trastevere. The tram stop where the walk began is immediately ahead.

APPENDIX

MORE WALKS FROM *ROME THE SECOND TIME:* *15 ITINERARIES THAT DON'T GO TO THE COLISEUM*

Rome the Second Time: 15 Itineraries That Don't Go to the Coliseum is available in paperback and most eBook formats. The paperback was published in 2009. The eBook was published in 2010 and has 200 hyperlinks and hyperlinked Google overlay maps. The eBook also hyperlinks to Updates to the book.

The 15 itineraries in *Rome the Second Time* are for the curious, adventurous traveler. They are itineraries you won't find elsewhere. Here's the Table of Contents of *Rome the Second Time*:

TABLE OF CONTENTS

PRAISE FOR *ROME THE SECOND TIME*

"Surprising, moving and extraordinary.... Makes me want to move back to Rome tomorrow." Patrizio Nissirio (Roman), International Correspondent, Ansa—Italian News Agency

"Passionate and intelligent—a rich and wonderful guidebook to unknown and under-discovered sites. Even after living in Italy for over 25 years, I found new information, new walks, and new discoveries in *Rome the Second Time*." Dana Prescott, Executive Director, Civitella Ranieri, Italy

"The fact that Walter Veltroni, the highly respected mayor of Rome until 2008 has written a foreword to this guidebook should inspire confidence in the *Transitions Abroad* reader eager to see the Rome behind the "Disneyland" itineraries, jammed with exhausted tourists that countless other guidebooks describe.... The authors take the reader through a number of itineraries, carefully explained and annotated with excellent maps." *Transitions Abroad* (www.transitionsabroad.com)

"This book is geared to the traveler who has already seen the big sights—the Coliseum, the Trevi Fountain, Vatican City and so on—and is ready to experience the less traveled, quirkier and definitely cheaper side of Rome. In other words, the Rome of ordinary people." *Chicago Tribune,* June Sawyers

"Most guidebooks are outdated by the time they reach the stores, but this one is different. Beautifully written, with an enthusiasm for the Eternal

City that warms every page, it takes readers far off the beaten path, into neighborhoods where tourists seldom tread." www.inromenow.com

"…if you're planning on staying in Rome for a while, or if you're coming back, there's a good argument that ROME THE SECOND TIME is the second guidebook you should buy.… If you're going to be in Rome for long enough, or regularly enough, to get past those first fevered days between the Coliseum and the Vatican, you may well want to dip into ROME THE SECOND TIME, and see what it has to offer. It's also supported by their Website, called, well, Rome the Second Time." www.romefile.com

MORE ABOUT THE AUTHORS

We—Bill Graebner and Dianne Bennett—met at Stanford-in-Italy in Florence. We continued our passion for Italy with sojourns, including to Dianne's relatives in Chiavenna, 15 kilometers south of the Swiss border. In 1989 we spent six months with our two sons in Bologna, immersed in that dark, mysterious medieval city, with its 40 kilometers of porticoes.

In 1993 Bill was awarded the Fulbright at *La Sapienza,* the University of Rome, where he taught U.S. history to Italians while Dianne explored the city on foot, inevitably yielding to its seductions. That year, we lived for six months near Piazza dei Re di Roma.

Dianne wanted to return to Rome regularly. Bill wasn't so sure. He offered a plan or, as Dianne remembers, an ultimatum. Yes, we could come back to Rome each year, but he wanted to live in a new neighborhood each time and to drive a scooter. Okay, said Dianne, you can have a scooter if you take motorcycle lessons, thinking that would deter him. It did not. After two days of lessons in the U.S., and a license in hand (Dianne got one too), we picked up a used Piaggio Hexagon in Bologna and drove it four days and more than 250 sometimes harrowing miles (over 400 kilometers) from Bologna, over the Apennines (on the famously curvy and dangerous La Futa) to Rome. Whew!

We began to return each year to Rome for anywhere from two weeks to three months, living in a new neighborhood each time, always outside the city's historic center.

We eventually wore the Piaggio into the ground. One day when we were exploring EUR, which became one of the walks in this book, the scooter stopped dead on via Cristoforo Colombo, in about six lanes of traffic. It was shortly to be retired anyway, because it did not meet new emission standards. How we disposed of it, what bureaucracy we did and did not deal with, is a story in itself.

We invested in a new, larger scooter—our current warhorse, a Bologna-made Malaguti Madison 250. And we continued to live in and explore different neighborhoods. We've found "our" coffee bar in San Giovanni, near Piazza dei Re di Roma; in Appio Latino, on the outskirts of Caffarella Park; in Monteverde Nuovo, twice, on both sides of Circonvallazione Gianicolense; in Trastevere, in a friend's art studio; in Trieste, just steps from Coppedè; in San Paolo, a block from Garbatella; in Flaminio, our apartment above the doorway where a bicycle was stolen in *The Bicycle Thief*; in Nomentano, in Piazza Bologna; in Monteverde Vecchio; and in Marconi.

We know enough Italian to read the daily newspaper, usually *La Repubblica,* and to parse the events around town—openings, exhibits, music, dance, readings, talks, political gatherings, and marches. With Italian hiking groups, we climb the gorgeous, often snow-capped mountains only one to two hours from Rome.

Both of us have written articles and books in our fields, Dianne in tax law, Bill in U.S. history. Bill started exploring links between U.S. and Italian history with an essay on the relationship between a Mussolini arch planned for E42 (see Walk 2) and the St. Louis Arch, "Gateway to Empire: An Interpretation of Eero Saarinen's 1948 Design for the St. Louis Arch." Bill's most popular book is *Coming of Age in Buffalo: Youth and Authority in the Postwar Era.* He is also the author of the highly-praised *Patty's Got a Gun.*

Rome the Second Time was the first book written together. Imagine that process! As we noted in the Introduction to that book, sometimes we just had to go with "he said/she said," because we couldn't possibly agree. These four new itineraries are another joint project, another effort at compromise and, for us, often a lot of slogging and hard work, sifting through thousands of photographs, checking and double-checking, in articles and books, in person and online, our Rome friends a trusted resource. In the end, a labor of love.

ABOUT THE BLOG

www.romethesecondtime.com is a blog we—Bill Graebner and Dianne Bennett—first developed as an adjunct to the book.

It took on a life of its own. We post on it every three to five days. Some of those posts are time sensitive, such as the review of an art exhibit or jazz performance. Others are history-focused, explorations in the meaning of the 1960 Olympics in Rome, or the Fascists' colonization efforts in Libya.

The blog's main topics are contemporary art (posts on the city's major contemporary museums or its avant-garde collectives); architecture, mainly 20th century (posts on l'ex GIL, the ex-youth center in Trastevere, and public housing); history, especially of the 19th and 20th centuries and with a focus on Fascism; social customs (posts on people choosing to walk in the streets and street art); sports, especially soccer; and politics (posts on election issues, on garbage collection and disposal). Although we are not foodies or shoppers, we sometimes write about a favorite restaurant, wine bar, local shop, the public markets, or an unusual item we find for sale. That we are deeply fond of Rome goes without saying, but we can be frustrated by it too; so there is an occasional post that laments the current state of the city, even what not to do in Rome. And now and then Dianne ventures into ancient and Renaissance history, with some "church lady" posts. We have linked sample posts in this paragraph.

The blog has its Top 40 as well: those 40 places in Rome we think deserve to be on the list for those viewing Rome the second—or umpteenth—time. You can see the Top 40 list at the right of the main post, and each listing links to the appropriate post. For those who can't wait, we can tell you the Gianicolo at night came in at No. 1 on our Top 40.

Readers of the books (*Rome the Second Time* and *Modern Rome*) will find new places to explore and more information about some of the places on the itineraries on www.romethesecondtime.com. Dianne did a series of posts on "homes" in Rome one can visit, including those of the artist Giorgio de Chirico and the novelist Alberto Moravia. Bill has written a number of posts explaining Rome's ubiquitous street art. So far, we haven't been at a loss for topics, though we welcome suggestions.

FACEBOOK

Rome the Second Time also is on Facebook, where we announce new posts. Michael Calleri, an admirer of the book, set up and manages the Facebook site, which often veers into matters other than those sparked by *RST*. We invite you to follow RST on Facebook.

RECOMMENDED ROME BLOGS

Weekly arts and culture updates:
  www.inromenow.com
  www.buzzinrome.com

Restaurant/food:
  www.parlafood.com
  www.elizabethminchilliinrome.com

Photography:
  www.romephotoblog.com

Contemporary art:
  www.facebook.com/ContempRomeSharaWasserman

Sustainable tourism:
  www.romefile.com

Italian politics and lifestyle:
  www.theamericanmag.com

General travel:
  www.goitaly.about.com

CPSIA information can be obtained
at www.ICGtesting.com
Printed in the USA
BVHW010411251118
533785BV00011B/258/P